The Book of Apollonius

The Book of
APOLLONIUS

TRANSLATED INTO ENGLISH VERSE

BY

RAYMOND L. GRISMER

AND

ELIZABETH ATKINS

UNIVERSITY OF MINNESOTA

THE UNIVERSITY OF MINNESOTA PRESS

MINNEAPOLIS

1936

COPYRIGHT, 1936, BY THE
UNIVERSITY OF MINNESOTA

LONDON : HUMPHREY MILFORD
OXFORD UNIVERSITY PRESS

PRINTED IN THE UNITED STATES OF AMERICA

Acknowledgments

We hereby wish to make grateful acknowledgment to Professor Douglas Bush and to Professor Marbury B. Ogle for suggestions regarding the bibliography of the Apollonius legend, and to Dr. John T. Flanagan for his critical reading of the manuscript.

Acknowledgment is also made to the Oxford University Press for permission to quote from Macaulay's edition of *The Complete Works of John Gower*.

R. L. G. and E. A.

Minneapolis, Minnesota
July, 1936

Introduction

This is a translation into English verse of the medieval Spanish poem, *El libro de Apolonio*. So far as the translators can ascertain, there is no other English translation of this important monument of Old Spanish literature, in either poetry or prose. The critical edition of Charles C. Marden, cited in the Bibliography below, has been used as the basis of the accompanying version.

THE APOLLONIUS LEGEND AND THE GREEK ROMANCE

The original treatment of the Apollonius theme belongs to that type of fictive literature known as the Greek romance. This form of narrative, cultivated by the Greek-speaking peoples of the Mediterranean, derives its popularity from its swift action and ever-changing scene. Endless variety of adventure and amazing journeys to the ends of the world bewilder the reader.

This type of literature probably originated in the story of the wanderings of Odysseus recounted by Homer, but as it developed it became more and more unrestrained. The travels of the characters of the Greek novel are no longer confined to the area of the Mediterranean basin. They pass boldly between the Pillars of Hercules and explore the uncharted seas. Not content with the limitations of the earth, they journey to other planets.

In Diogenes' *The Incredible Things That Happened beyond Thule* the hero Dinias visits Thule, probably the islands north of Scotland, reaches the vicinity of the North Pole, and even travels around the earth. Not to be outdone, the heroine Dercyllis, who, like Apollonius, is a citizen of Tyre, visits the underworld and later lives in a land of Amazons. Her brother Mantinia surpasses their records with trips to the sun and the moon. Weary from their travels the three are at last reunited in the city of Tyre, where they settle down to a peaceful existence. The constant references to Tyre connect the novel with the literature dealing with Apollonius, king of that city. Moreover, Diogenes makes use of an old literary trick when he claims that the story is not his but one found in Tyre by Alexander the Great. So, too, did Cervantes claim to have bought the unsurpassed account of the adventures of Don Quijote and Sancho Panza from a boy selling pamphlets on a street corner of Toledo! Numerous variations of this device may be found in the Spanish novels of chivalry, which are a definite outgrowth of the Greek romance.

But the journeys taken by the hero and heroine are no idle travels prompted by curiosity. The principal characters of the novels are fleeing from cruel enemies who pursue them relentlessly through an endless series of adventures. In the *Babylonica* of Iamblichus the girl Sinonis, fleeing from the Babylonian king, is attacked by a demon, poisoned by the honey of venomous bees, accused of murder, buried alive, captured, drugged, and wooed by a wealthy merchant, whom she murders while he is intoxicated. She even tries to commit suicide by stabbing herself. Her lover Rhodanes is no less persecuted, finally being crucified by the jealous king. He survives this misadventure, however, to live to marry Sinonis and supplant the monarch who had caused the lovers so many tribulations.

An Aethiopian History or *Theagenes and Chariclea* by Heliodorus is a typical example of a Greek novel in which extensive use is made of pirates. Capture by pirates enables Chariclea to escape marriage with Alcamenus, but she immediately becomes a cause of strife between the leaders of the outlaws. In the general fight that ensues all the pirates are killed except one, who flees. But Chariclea has little time to congratulate herself on her deliverance, for she and her lover are straightway captured by pirates from Egypt. This device of capture by bandits appears constantly in the Greek romances and reappears in *The Book of Apollonius,* where Tarsiana is saved from an assassin by the timely arrival of pirates from the sea. (See quatrains 385 ff.)

The shipwrecks that play so large a part in the adventures of Apollonius are also a stock device of the Greek romance. In the *Leucippe and Clitophon* of Achilles Tatius, the name characters flee from the city of Tyre and are shipwrecked off the coast of Egypt in the general locality where Apollonius "strayed, a palmer." (See quatrain 360.)

Even Luciana's burial at sea and subsequent revival when her coffin floated ashore at Ephesus has its parallel in Greek romance. The heroine of Chariton's *Chaereas and Callirrhoe* faints and, after being buried, revives when the grave is broken into by pirates in quest of treasure. Similarly Anthia, of Xenophon's *Ephesiaca* or *Habrocomas and Anthia,* is entombed after taking a sleeping potion but is rescued by pirates in search of loot.

LATIN VERSIONS OF THE APOLLONIUS LEGEND

There are references to the story of Apollonius in Latin works of the sixth, seventh, eighth, and ninth centuries.[*] The

[*] Marden, *Libro de Apolonio,* I, xxii–xxiv.

early Latin versions were translations from the Greek, if we may judge from the Greek words used and the Greek customs described. We have preserved to us from the tenth century a manuscript containing a Latin redaction entitled *Historia Apollonii regis Tyri.* This manuscript (No. LXVI-4) is now in the Laurentian Library of Florence and was printed in Germany about 1475 without date or place of publication, by Marcus Welser in 1595, by Lapaume, Paris, in 1856, and by Alexander Riese, Leipzig, in 1871, 1892, 1893, and 1899.

There were more than fifty of these manuscripts, which vary widely. An eleventh-century manuscript entitled the *Gesta Apollonii* is preserved in the University Library of Ghent and was published by Dümmler in 1888 in his *Poetae Latinae aevi Carolini* (II, 483–506).

A late eleventh-century Latin version is the *Pantheon* (or *Universal Chronicle*) of Godfrey of Viterbo, printed in 1726 and included in 1895 by S. Singer in his *Apollonius aus Tyrus,* etc. (see the Bibliography), pp. 150–77.

The last Latin version of importance is included in the fourteenth-century *Gesta Romanorum,* printed by A. Keller, Stuttgart, in 1842, by H. Oesterley, Berlin, in 1872, and in S. Singer, *op. cit.,* pp. 68–105, in 1895.

THE SOURCES OF THE SPANISH POEM

The source of the Spanish *Libro de Apolonio* was some medieval Latin version of the *Historia Apollonii regis Tyri,* probably not that of the Florentine manuscript and certainly not that of the manuscript preserved in the Bodleian Library at Oxford. Of the versions available for comparison, the Florentine *Historia* seems closest; possibly it was a copy of this manuscript that was the immediate source of the Spanish poem. The sequence of events and the details of the descriptions are the same in the Latin and Spanish versions. There is also close verbal similarity, particularly in the forms of proper names, which have varied greatly in the different treatments of the legend. Finally, verse 372b, *Catat lo en la estoria si a mi no creyedes,* seems to be a direct reference of the poet to the *estoria* he was following.

A POSSIBLE SOURCE IN OLD FRENCH OR PROVENZAL LITERATURE

Many have claimed some vague source for the Spanish poem in Old French and Provenzal. It is true that there are references to the Apollonius legend in the *Aye d'Avignon, Poème Moral, Doon de Nantueil, Roman del 'Escoufle, Philomena,* and Gui de Cambrai's *Balaham et Josaphas.** But these references, while they indicate familiarity with the theme, do not prove that there were French poems dealing with Apollonius. A single fragment of fifty-two verses found by Alfred Schulze† in 1909 does not prove the existence of an Old French epic antedating the *Libro de Apolonio.* Almost all the details of the story are entirely different, and, more significant still, not a single rhyme of the Old French fragment appears in the Spanish poem. The earliest extant versions in Old French are six manuscript prose translations of the *Historia Apollonii regis Tyri,* all dating from the fourteenth and fifteenth centuries.

Formerly many words of the *Libro de Apolonio* were thought to be Provenzal, but it has been proved that they are old Aragonese forms and indicate that one of the copyists was from Aragon. There are early references to Apollonius in

* Marden, *op. cit.,* I, xxviii–xxix.
† "Ein Bruchstück des altfranzösischen Apolloniusromans," *Zeitschrift für romanische Philologie,* 33:226–29.

Provenzal literature by Guiraut de Cabreira, Bertran de Paris, Guilhem Arnaut de Marsan, King Pedro IV of Aragon, and others. No poems have been found, however, that might have furnished the material for the Spanish poem.

THE DATE OF EL LIBRO DE APOLONIO

The lost original of the Spanish *Libro de Apolonio* dates from the first half of the thirteenth century.* It takes an important place among the extant pieces of Old Spanish literature, *El poema de mio Cid, El poema de Fernan Gonzalez, El libro de Alexandre,* and the poems of Gonzalo de Berceo. These works date from the twelfth and thirteenth centuries and form one of the most brilliant collections of early poetry in any language.

Heretofore the poem has always been dated by comparing words and phrases of the *Apolonio* with similar ones in other poems of this group. A possible addition to the evidence already presented may be found in the *Grande e general estoria* (1270). The historians working under the direction of Alfonso X (El Sabio) end Book IV with the promise:

> *E comiença se la quinta parte desta ystoria en el rey apolonio.*

Book V has been lost, and it is impossible to know whether the compilers of the early Spanish history used the *Libro de Apolonio* or some prose history in Latin on the same theme.

THE MANUSCRIPT

The Spanish poem has been preserved in a single manuscript, No. III-K-4 of the library of the Escorial. It measures 250 by 180 mm., and is in the handwriting of a copyist of the

---
* Mérimée and Morley, *History of Spanish Literature*, p. 45.

fourteenth century.* Of the three poems contained in the manuscript, *El libro de Apolonio,* which is the first, occupies folios 1r to 64v, inclusive.

THE AUTHOR

The anonymous author of the Spanish poem we may assume to have been a cleric, not because he writes in the *mester de clerecía* (*vide infra*), for that poetic school included all educated writers, but rather because he sermonizes constantly, a feature that renders certain passages of the poem tiresome to many. Moreover, he begins the poem "En el nombre de Dios e de Santa Maria" and ends with "Amen Deus."

THE POETIC FORM OF THE SPANISH POEM

El libro de Apolonio is one of the first examples of the *nueua maestria* (see verse 1c), known as *mester de clerecía* or "[poetic] art of the clergy." It was the purpose of the latter to diffuse among the Christians of Spain a knowledge of the lives of the saints and of the miracles of the Virgin, favorite medieval themes. But the subject matter was not always religious. Sometimes a pagan like Alexander the Great was the central figure, sometimes a local hero like Fernán González.

The verse form used by the new school is a monorhymed quatrain with fourteen syllables in each line. This type of versification is known as *cuaderna vía* and consists of four Alexandrines with a single rhyme. Each line is divided into hemistichs of seven syllables each, with the last stress on the sixth and thirteenth syllables. In the hands of a less skillful poet than the anonymous author of the *Libro de Apolonio* the long lines of the *cuaderna vía* become heavy and the monorhyme proves monotonous.

---

* Marden, *op. cit.,* I, ix, xii–xix.

THE MERIT OF THE SPANISH POEM

"It is one of the earliest examples of the *nueva maestría* and likewise one of the most curious and best written."* Considering its antiquity, this version is notable for complexity of plot, the delineation of the characters, and the inventiveness of the poet. The poem is essentially narrative though there are lyric passages of beauty.

THE COPYIST

There is abundant evidence of the carelessness of the fourteenth-century copyist, for many words are erased and rewritten, others are blotted, and not a few have been copied from above or below into lines where obviously they do not belong. Over fifteen hundred verses do not have the correct number of syllables, six stanzas (62, 67, 196, 516, 598, and 604) lack a verse, and one stanza (102) has one verse too many. Moreover, there are numerous instances of bad rhyme, many of which are obviously errors of the copyist.

OTHER VERSIONS OF THE APOLLONIUS LEGEND IN SPANISH LITERATURE

There were few reworkings of the Apollonius theme in Spanish literature. It is interesting to note that the legend next came to Spain from England via Portugal. Late in the fourteenth century a Portuguese, Roberto Payn(a), translated part of John Gower's *Confessio Amantis*. (See page xv below.) A few years later the Portuguese translation was turned into Castilian by Juan de Cuenca. The manuscript is preserved in the library of the Escorial (No. G-II-19) and was published by Adolf Birch-Hirschfeld, Leipzig, in 1909. The 1858 catalog of the library of the Escorial lists the translation as:

* Mérimée and Morley, *op. cit.*, p. 45.

Confision del amante, libro así intitulado compuesto por Joan Goer natural del Reyno de Englaterra e tornado en lengua Portuguesa por Roberto Payn ó Payna canónigo de la ciudad de Lisboa e después fué puesto en lenguaje castellano por Juan de Cuenca natural de Huete. Cod. escrito en papel el año de 1400, fol. menor, pasta.

The next Spanish reworking, the *Historia de los Siete Sabios y del rey Apolonio* (Sevilla, 1495), has been lost, so that we cannot determine whether it bore any relation to the *Libro de Apolonio*. It is certain that the story of Apollonius which is the subject of *patraña* No. 11 of Juan de Timoneda's *Patrañuelo* (Valencia, 1576) is not related to any other Spanish version. Many names are different and other details are changed. It probably was taken directly from a manuscript of the *Historia*, possibly from the Viennese manuscript.

THE LEGEND IN ENGLISH LITERATURE

The Apollonius legend figures prominently in English literature, one of the earliest extant translations into Anglo-Saxon being a fragment of the *Historia Apollonii regis Tyri*. In the fourteenth century John Gower included the story of Apollonius in his *Confessio Amantis* (Book VIII). Gower drew material from the *Historia* and from the *Pantheon*,* adapting the episodes to suit his own purpose, as the "analysis" will show:

Apollonius of Tyre. In a Chronicle called Pantheon I read how king Antiochus ravished his daughter and lived with her in sin. To hinder her marriage, he proposed a problem to those who sought her love, and if a man failed to resolve it, he must lose his head. At length came the Prince Apollinus of Tyre, and the king proposed to him the question. He saw too clearly what the riddle

* See Singer, *Apollonius aus Tyrus,* pp. 153-77; Macaulay, *Complete Works of John Gower,* III, 536-37.

meant, and Antiochus fearing shame put off the time of his reply for thirty days. (271–439.)

The Prince feared his vengeance and fled home to Tyre, and thence he departed secretly in a ship laden with wheat. Antiochus sent one Taliart in all haste to Tyre, with command to make away with the Prince by poison. Finding that Apollinus had fled, he returned.

In the meantime the Prince came to Tharsis, and took lodging there with one Strangulio and his wife Dionise. The city was suffering famine, and Apollinus gave them his wheat as a free gift, in return for which they set up a statue of him in the common place. (440–570.)

A man came to him from Tyre and reported that king Antiochus desired to slay him. He was afraid and fled thence again by ship. A storm came upon him and the ship was wrecked: Apollinus alone came alive to land. A fisherman helped him and directed him to the town of Pentapolim, where he found the people gathered to see games, and the king and queen of the country there present. (571–695.)

He surpassed all others in the games, and the king called him to supper in his hall. At supper he was sad and ate nothing, and the king sent to him his daughter to console him. To her he told his name and country, and with that he let the tears run down his cheeks. She fetched a harp and sang to it, and he took it from her hand and played and sang divinely. They all saw that he was of gentle blood. (696–799.)

The king's daughter desired her father that he might be her teacher, and in the course of time she turned with all her heart to love of him. She so lost her appetite for meat and drink and sleep that she was in danger of her life.

Three sons of princes demanded her in marriage, and she by letter informed her father how the matter stood: if she might not have Apollinus, she would have none other. (800–911.)

The king sent for Apollinus and showed him his daughter's letter. He assented gladly, and the marriage took place with great festivity. Soon after this men came from Tyre reporting that Antiochus and his daughter were dead, having been both struck by lightning, and entreating him to return to his own people. All were rejoiced to hear that the king's daughter had married so worthy a prince. (912–1019.)

Apollinus sailed away with his wife, she being with child. A storm arose and she began to be in travail. In anguish she was delivered of a maid child, but she herself lay dead. (1020–1058.)

Apollinus sorrowed as never man sorrowed before, but the master of the ship required that the dead body be cast out of the ship, because the sea will not hold within itself any dead creature, and the ship would be driven on the shore if the body remained within her. They made therefore a coffer closely bound with iron and covered with pitch, in which they placed the corpse, with gold and jewels, and with a letter praying that she might receive burial; and so they cast it overboard. Apollinus in the meantime sailed first to Tharsis. (1059–1150.)

The coffer was cast up at Ephesim and was found by Cerymon, a great physician. He by his art restored the seeming corpse to life, and she took upon herself the rule of religion and dwelt with other women in the temple of Diane. (1151–1271.)

Apollinus coming to Tharsis entrusted his infant daughter Thaise to the care of Strangulio and Dionise, and so he sailed on to Tyre. This daughter, until she was fourteen years old, grew up with the daughter of Strangulio, but Thaise was preferred to the other in all places where they went, and Dionise was therefore wroth. She bade her bondman Theophilus take Thaise down to the shore of the sea and there slay her. He brought her to the sea, but her cry called forth pirates from their hiding-place, who carried her with them away to Mitelene and sold her to Leonin, master of a brothel. (1272–1423.)

The young men who came to her were moved by compassion and did her no wrong, so that Leonin sent his own servant in to her. She entreated to be permitted to make gain for him in some other way, and being taken from the brothel and placed in security, she taught such things as gentlewomen desire to learn, and her name went forth over all the land. (1424–1497.)

Theophilus reported that he had slain Thaise, and Dionise, pretending that she had died suddenly, made a great funeral and set up a tomb with an epitaph. After this, Apollinus came to seek for this daughter at Tharsis, and hearing that she was dead, he put forth to sea again in grievous sorrow. He lay weeping alone in the darkness of the ship's hold, until under stress of storm they came to Mitelene. (1498–1617.)

Hearing of his grief, the lord of the city, Athenagoras, sent Thaise to comfort him. He at first rejected all her consolation, but then to his joy discovered that she was the daughter for whom he mourned. Athenagoras asked for her in marriage and was wedded to her. (1618–1776.)

They went forth all together with intent to avenge the treason at Tharsis, but Apollinus was warned in a dream to go to Ephesim, and there in the temple of Diane he found the wife whom he supposed to have been dead. Thence they voyaged to Tyre and were received with joy. Athenagoras and Thaise were there crowned king and queen, and Apollinus sailed away and took due vengeance upon Strangulio and Dionise. (1777–1962.)

When this was done, a letter came to him from Pentapolim, praying him to come and receive that kingdom, since the king was dead. They had a good voyage thither, and he and his wife were crowned there and led their life happily. (1963–2008.) *

The octosyllabic couplet that Gower chose as the metrical form for his work was again used by Shakespeare in his treatment of this legend, in *Pericles,* when he put the story of Apollonius into the mouth of Gower in the prologues of each of the five acts and at the end of the play. For this reason the present translators have chosen a similar verse form as the appropriate English meter for this translation.

Gower's poem, finished about 1390 and printed by Caxton as early as 1483, was followed by Robert Copland's prose romance *Kynge Appolyn of Thyre* (1510) and a prose transla-

---

* Macaulay, *op. cit.,* II, lxxxvii–lxxxix.

tion of the story from the *Gesta Romanorum, The Patterne of Painefulle Aduenters* (1576) by Laurence Twine. Shakespeare took the plot of his *Pericles, Prince of Tyre* from Gower's poem, but he was also familiar with prose versions of the legend current in and before his time. A year before Shakespeare's *Pericles* was printed, there appeared a novel based partly on Twine's prose work and partly on the play *The Painful Adventures of Pericles Prince of Tyre. Being the true History of the Play of Pericles, as it was lately presented by the worthy and ancient Poet John Gower. At London: Printed by T. P. for Nat. Butler, 1608.* The material borrowed from Shakespeare's play must have been taken down in shorthand at one of the performances of the *Pericles*. Later English reworkings of the theme are George Wilkins' prose romance *The Painful Aduentures of Pericles, Prince of Tyre* (1608) and George Lillo's play *Marina* (1738), the name-character of the latter being taken from Shakespeare's play.

In Germany there are references to the Apollonius legend as early as the twelfth century, but the principal use of the theme occurs in Heinrich von Neustadt's fourteenth-century epic *Apollonius von Tyrland,* based on the *Historia Apollonii regis Tyri.* The legend was also popular in Holland, Denmark, Sweden, Iceland, Hungary, and Italy.

Selected Bibliography

BAIST, GOTTFRIED. "Die spanische Literatur." *Grundriss der romanischen Philologie,* II, 2. Strassburg, 1901.

CHARITON. *Le avventure di Cherea e Calliroe, romanzo tradotto da Aristide Calderini.* Torino, 1913.

CHENERY, WINTHROP HOLT. "Object Pronouns in Dependent Clauses: A Study of Old Spanish Word Order." *Publications of the Modern Language Association,* 20:1–151 (1905).

DUNLOP, JOHN COLIN. *History of Prose Fiction,* Vol. 1. London, 1911.

HAGEN, HERMANN. *Der Roman vom König Apollonius von Tyrus in seinen verschiedenen Bearbeitungen.* Berlin, 1878.

HANSSEN, FEDERICO. "Sobre la conjugación del *Libre de Apolonio.*" *Anales de la Universidad de Chile,* 41:637–55 (1896).

HAUPT, MORITZ. "Über die Erzählung von Apollonius aus Tyrus." *Opuscula,* Vol. 3. Leipzig, 1876.

HELIODORUS OF EMESA. *An Aethiopian History Written in Greek by Heliodorus. Englished by Thomas Underdowne, anno 1587.* London, 1895.

KLEBS, ELIMAR. *Die Erzählung von Apollonius aus Tyrus. Eine geschichtliche Untersuchung über ihre lateinische Urform und ihre späteren Bearbeitungen.* Berlin, 1899.

LEWIS, C. B. "Die altfranzösischen Prosaversionen des Appollonius-Romans." *Romanische Forschungen,* 34, Heft 1, pp. 1–277. Erlangen, 1913.

MACAULAY, GEORGE CAMPBELL. *The Complete Works of John Gower,* Vols. II, III. Oxford, 1901.

MARDEN, CHARLES CARROLL. *Libro de Apolonio.* Part I: *Text and Introduction,* Baltimore, 1917; Part II, *Grammar, Notes, and Vocabulary,* Princeton, 1922.

—— "Notes on the Text of the *Libre d' Apolonio.*" *Modern Language Notes,* 18:18–20 (1903).

—— "Unos trozos oscuros del *Libro de Apolonio.*" *Revista de Filología Española,* 3:290–97 (1916).

MENÉNDEZ Y PELAYO, MARCELINO. *Antología de poetas líricos castellanos,* 2:lviii–lxi. Madrid, 1912.

MÉRIMÉE, ERNEST, and SYLVANUS GRISWOLD MORLEY. *History of Spanish Literature.* New York, 1930.

MILÁ Y FONTANALS, MANUEL. *De la poesía heroico-popular castellana.* Barcelona, 1874.

NEUSTADT, HEINRICH VON. *Apollonius von Tyrland.* Berlin, 1906.

PIDAL, PEDRO JOSÉ. "Vidas del Rey Apolonio y Santa María Egipciaca y la Adoración de los Santos Reyes." *Revista de Madrid,* Vol. 4 (1840). Also in *Estudios literarios,* 1:151–67, 169–89. Madrid, 1890.

PUYMAIGRE, THÉODORE JOSEPH BOUDET, COMTE DE. *Vieux auteurs castillans,* 1:229–50. Madrid, 1888.

SCHULZE, ALFRED. "Ein Bruchstück des altfranzösischen Apolloniusromans," *Zeitschrift für romanische Philologie,* 33:226–29.

SINGER, SAMUEL. *Apollonius aus Tyrus. Untersuchung über das Fortleben des antiken Romans in spätern Zeiten.* Halle a. S., 1895.

—— *Aufsätze und Vorträge,* pp. 79–103. Tübingen, 1912.

SMYTH, ALBERT H. *Shakespeare's "Pericles" and Apollonius of Tyre: A Study in Comparative Literature.* Philadelphia, 1898.

THORPE, BENJAMIN. *The Anglo-Saxon Version of the Story of Apollonius of Tyre.* London, 1834.

WOLFF, SAMUEL LEE. *The Greek Romances in Elizabethan Prose Fiction.* New York, 1912.

The Book of Apollonius

The Book of Apollonius

The Book of Apollonius

1 In God's and Holy Mary's name,
  If they will guide, it is my aim
  In a new style of poetry
  To tell of a king's courtesy.

2 King Apollonius of Tyre
  Lost queen and child through evils dire,
  But, through his long fidelity,
  He won them both back finally.

3 But now I will my tale begin
  With Antioch's first sovereign,
  Antiochus. After he built
  His great seaport, he turned to guilt.

4 For after while his consort died
  And left a daughter at his side.
  A maid could not be lovelier;
  No flaw was anywhere on her.

5 But though great princes crossed the sea
  To marry her, that might not be,
  For something chanced which was so shameful
  That even to speak of it is blameful.

6　The devil, who is never quiet,
　　Caused King Antiochus' blood to riot
　　In lust. He loved his child so well
　　That he lost all his fear of hell.

7　This sin bred worse sin without measure,
　　For with his child he took his pleasure—
　　Yea, robbed her of virginity,
　　Forcing her most unwillingly.

8　Shame caused her then to moan and cry;
　　She touched no food, that she might die;
　　But her old nurse, to ease her shame,
　　Kept saying she was not to blame.

9　"Daughter," she said, "you are dismayed
　　By something you could not evade.
　　What happened was your destiny.
　　Grieve not for what was bound to be.

10　"And now to my advice take heed.
　　 Do not reveal your father's deed.
　　 Your own ill fame would be the fruit
　　 Of bringing him to disrepute."

11　"Nurse," said the girl, "this should not be.
　　 My sire's love is my misery.
　　 His daughter, can that still be I?
　　 Nameless is now our family tie.

12 "Yet naught can cure my violation.
   Good nurse, I'll heed your exhortation.
   I was forsaken by the Lord.
   I will respect your counseling word."

13 I know the devil possessed the king.
   He ignored the vileness of this thing.
   God loathed the ways in which he went,
   But he cared not for God's content.

14 To keep his child unwedded still,
   That he might do his wicked will,
   He played a trick most grossly evil,
   Inspired by that foul beast, the devil.

15 Lest he incur an evil stigma,
   The king made an obscure enigma.
   Who guessed it might the daughter wed,
   Who guessed it not must lose his head.

16 This caused so many heads to fall
   That they trimmed all the city wall.
   Folk feared the girl as a sorceress nearly,
   For she cost noble youths so dearly.

17 "The branch's leaf is like the root.
   The father eats the mother's fruit."
   The man who saw what this could mean
   Might have the princess for his queen.

18 When Apollonius, king of Tyre,
   Heard this girl was all men's desire,
   He longed to marry her, although
   He doubted fate would have it so.

19 He came to Antioch's seaport,
   Greeted the king and all the court,
   And asked to wed the girl by law,
   And Tyre as bride-gift she would draw.

20 In court were men who loved the truth.
   It grieved them much to see this youth
   Who nothing knew of dealings sly
   And hence by sorcery must die.

21 The assembled court he then addressed
   And made his purpose manifest.
   The king posed this alternative:
   The answer or his head he'd give.

22 Now Apollonius was well versed
   In riddles; therefore from the first
   Of the king's sin he was as sure
   As if he saw his acts impure.

23 He wished himself in another land.
   Imprudent 'twas to understand;
   And yet lest he should seem unlearned,
   He spoke the answer he discerned.

24 He said, "This riddle is unfair.
   It brings all guessers shame and care.
   If its dark words are plainly said,
   They mean you take your child to bed.

25 "You are the root, your child the tree.
   In mortal sin through her you be.
   Your child inherits the fleshly act
   Her mother did in marriage pact."

26 Though this was what the king had asked,
   He raged because he was unmasked.
   His lust was driving him insane.
   He longed to have this suitor slain.

27 He said, his foul crime to disguise,
   That Apollonius uttered lies,
   And not for worlds that deed he'd do.
   But the court thought the answer true.

28 He ruled his guest must lose his head,
   Since the riddle was not rightly read,
   But he would grant him thirty days
   To solve the riddle in other ways.

29 Apollonius fled away
   Before that fatal thirtieth day.
   In his deep grief his one desire
   Was to return with speed to Tyre.

30 With joy his people met their king.
    They thronged about him triumphing.
    They thanked the Lord, both great and small,
    Townsfolk, villagers, and all.

31 Apollonius shut himself away
    And read his books day after day.
    He read all riddles and tales of men
    In Chaldean and Latin, again and again.

32 And in the end he could not see
    How to read that riddle differently.
    Therefore at last he ceased to read.
    He found no help in his sore need.

33 He told himself he had small skill
    To lose the lady and fare so ill.
    He pondered thus till he became
    Bowed with worry and with shame.

34 He felt a deep humiliation;
    He could not bear his degradation,
    But filled his ships with food and treasures
    That he might seek adventurous pleasures.

35 He sailed in secret with few men.
    Only his servants knew it then.
    On a favoring wind the swift ship rode.
    He soon reached Tarsus, and there abode.

36 Now let us seek Antiochus
   For we must not neglect him thus.
   He hated Apollonius madly
   And would have killed him very gladly.

37 Talliarchus was his favorite.
   What he advised, the king thought right,
   And kept him at his own right hand,
   And now he gave him this command:

38 The king said, "Listen, loyal brother,
   To something I would tell no other.
   For now with you I must discuss
   How to kill Apollonius.

39 "What I have done he has made known.
   No man has dared but he alone.
   He feels safe, since the world is big,
   And thinks I'm just a withered twig.

40 "I'll give you any boon you need
   If you go to Tyre, and go with speed;
   Kill him by poison or kill him by sword,
   And you may name your own reward."

41 Then Talliarchus was not slow.
   To please his lord he hastened to go.
   He planned to seek the king of Tyre
   And offer himself to him for hire.

42 But Tyre was filled with moans and crying.
　　Men rent their robes, and all were sighing.
　　There was sound of sobbing instead of song.
　　Churches were filled with a praying throng.

43 He saw that they had undergone
　　Ill fortune that had made them wan.
　　He asked the men what heavy blow
　　Made them appear half dead with woe.

44 A good man answered, "It is clear
　　That you live far away from here.
　　For you would weep as much, or more,
　　If you had lived upon our shore.

45 "The king who used to govern us,
　　Whose name was Apollonius,
　　Desired Antiochus' daughter.
　　He was the noblest man who sought her.

46 "Antiochus made excuse and cheated,
　　And Apollonius was defeated,
　　And so came home without the bride.
　　Shame now drives him far and wide.

47 "Our king was God's own gift to us.
　　Peerless was Apollonius.
　　Now, losing him, we are unmanned,
　　For hapless is a kingless land!"

48 This news made Talliarchus blissful.
   He felt his mission was successful.
   He went back to Antiochus
   To tell that things had happened thus.

49 He told his king he need not fret,
   For his foe was fleeing before his threat.
   Antiochus said, "He cannot flee
   To town or desert safe from me."

50 Then was a proclamation read:
   For Apollonius, live or dead,
   The king would give wealth all unstinted,
   And a hundred talents, freshly minted.

51 May God confound that wicked creature
   Possessed of such an evil nature
   That he a truthful man would kill,
   Who solved a riddle with such skill!

52 The devil was to blame for this,
   And he makes others do amiss.
   He tempts a man day after day.
   The Scriptures show his steady way.

53 A man, to hide some slight defection,
   Tells a lie, without reflection.
   Yet perjury is foe of Faith;
   Hark what the Law of Heaven saith:

54 All sins are but a single bane;
   They are like a tangled skein.
   Unless the first is soon corrected,
   All a man's morals are deflected.

55 That makes me of a hermit think.
   The devil tempted him with drink.
   Adultery next was the sin he tried.
   And his last sin was homicide.

56 So too Antiochus' first mistake
   Drove him a greater one to make.
   If for his first he had felt remorse,
   He had not embarked on an evil course.

57 In the old saw 'tis wisely spoken:
   "It is by greed a bag is broken."
   The king's reward made many stir
   To take our hero prisoner.

58 From greed grows many another sin.
   In order this reward to win
   Men did not hide their great desire
   To kill Apollonius, king of Tyre.

59 Many a man who was once his friend
   Was now turned foe, and sought his end.
   May God confound this world, if we
   Love pennies more than loyalty!

60 Antiochus ordered ships of wood
    To sail as quickly as they could,
    All filled with soldiers, arms, and grain.
    But God frustrated him again.

61 God does not like men's sinful pride,
    So all their plans He set aside.
    He hid Apollonius from the sword.
    Bless we and praise we such a Lord!

62 I wish to leave Antiochus.
    I wish to treat Apollonius.
    Remember in Tarsus still he was.

63 In Tarsus he, with grief-bowed head,
    Had anchors dropped in the roadstead.
    It seemed a place to leave the ship
    And rest from the long ocean trip.

64 His seamen then built bonfires hot.
    They fried and boiled in pan and pot.
    The meal's variety was great.
    'Twas served on priceless cloths and plate.

65 To men on shore who sniffed their meat
    They freely gave all they could eat.
    Hence the shore-dwellers liked them well,
    And of their need began to tell.

66 The crops were small and prices great;
   A single meal that one child ate
   Was worth a dollar. It cost three
   To feed a ploughman properly.

67 Apollonius had so wise a head
   That by all he was visited.
   And all were pleased with what he said.

68 Elanicus came. Gray-haired was he,
   An old man of good family.
   He led Apollonius by the hand
   To a flat and lonely meadowland.

69 He said that he was very sad
   For he had learned news that was bad:
   "Oh noble king, you do not know
   That you have heavy cause for woe.

70 "Antiochus' rage you have called down.
   No one will lodge you, in village or town.
   Whoever kills you will be paid.
   You'll lose your life, I am afraid."

71 The king then said in rage and pain,
   "For God's sake, good man, make it plain
   Why my life should be at stake.
   And how much will my murderer make?"

72 "The king would kill you, certainly,
   Because he's what you wished to be.
   One hundred talents he has said
   He'll give the one who brings your head."

73 Apollonius said, "No crime I willed
   Makes him give order I be killed.
   But I must trust in God, my strength,
   Who gives the afflicted help at length.

74 "To you, who thus the news reveal,
   Friendship and gratitude I feel.
   Now take as much gold as the king
   Would pay you for my murdering.

75 "Take it, in safety, without sin,
   Because my helper you have been.
   Else you'd have cause for blaming me
   Because you lost the killer's fee."

76 The good man sweetly answered, "King,
   I thank you for your offering,
   But if I took it, I'd do ill;
   In our land friends don't sell good will."

77 Let Christians pray that God may grant
   Such friends to them in their great want.
   And if a friend like this God give,
   Praise him now, while he still doth live.

78 Elanicus, fearful of suspicion,
   Since he came on this friendly mission,
   Sobbing, from the king then went,
   And in his grief his robes he rent.

79 The king remained to meditate.
   He now was in a sorry state,
   With many men after him seeking,
   Ready to slay him, awake or sleeping.

80 Pondering thus, and very sad,
   He saw a citizen richly clad:
   Strangilus he, wealthy and wise.
   The king besought him to advise.

81 "I wish," he said, "to speak to you,
   To ask you what I am to do.
   Antiochus' hirelings come to kill me.
   How to escape from them, now tell me.

82 "If you would help me now to hide,
   I might with you a while reside.
   If the council grant this my behest,
   To Tarsus I'll make rich bequest."

83 Strangilus knew he was a king.
   He said, "We cannot do this thing.
   We are too poor to give to you
   All that to your great rank is due.

84 "But let me learn of you one thing.
   Why did you quarrel with Antioch's king?
   None will shield you from that hater
   Unless it be our great Creator."

85 Then Apollonius replied,
   "His deep-loved child I sought as bride.
   I solved the riddle that was disputed.
   Therefore I am persecuted.

86 "Another point I would make clear.
   You say your town can't have me here.
   But if you aid me you will gain
   One hundred thousand bushels of grain.

87 "I will charge for it no higher
   Than I paid for it in Tyre.
   I'll then return the price, in pity,
   To help you fortify your city."

88 Strangilus was then elate.
   He kissed the king's hands, lay prostrate.
   "Welcome, King Apollonius,"
   He cried, "In need you succored us!

89 "And now I make a pact with you
   To bind ourselves in friendship true.
   Our men will pledge to save your life
   Or die with you in any strife."

90 Strangilus set about the act
   To please the king with this strange pact.
   He ordered heralds to repeat
   That the council now must meet.

91 The council met, and Strangilus
   Gave his command. All answered thus:
   "It is but just that we should give
   Such men our worship while they live."

92 Then Apollonius kept his word.
   The starved were fed; death was deferred.
   To all the city he was savior.
   This was a saintly man's behavior.

93 Great are God's grace and holiness.
   He always aids men in distress,
   And always takes away their grief.
   May we be steadfast in belief.

94 God chastens men to make them fear Him;
   Despite their sins, He draws men near Him.
   He makes all men confess Him master;
   He gives men joy; He gives disaster.

95 Apollonius now had earned
   The love of all men, and they yearned
   To entertain him as their guest.
   By lords and peasants he was blest.

96 And now to give him greater honor,
   They made a sculpture for their donor.
   It said, "To Apollonius
   For benefits he gave to us."

97 They raised it in the marketplace,
   Setting it on a lofty base.
   Till the end of all mortality
   This will be held in memory.

98 In Tarsus he remained among
   The happy, grateful people long.
   One host advised him to do this:
   To winter at Pentapolis.

99 "Believe me, king," said Strangilus,
   " 'Tis best that I advise you thus.
   By visiting Pentapolis
   You will give that city bliss.

100 "Rumors will spread on land and sea
    That you are here; and presently
    Antiochus will hear them, and
    His armies will besiege our land.

101 "Of food, you know, we have no store.
    We cannot stand besieging war.
    Nor will a full surrender shield
    Us, for they'll kill us though we yield.

102 "But if you flee, Antiochus
   Will tell his soldiers to disband,
   And you'll come back then to this land.
   And we shall all win safety thus."
   "You are wise," said Apollonius.

103 On shipboard then they loaded wine
   And bread and dried flesh of the kine.
   And they hired skillful mariners
   Who knew each shifting wind that stirs.

104 Now Apollonius could stay
   No longer, and he sailed away.
   The folk of Tarsus watched till he
   Was hidden by the widening sea.

105 All wept with him; all seemed to grieve
   That there was need for him to leave.
   They begged him swiftly to return.
   Of such pure love I'm pleased to learn.

106 Ill-omened was the time of going.
   Stern though favoring winds were blowing.
   The folk of Tarsus watched each sail
   Till distance made their eyesight fail.

107 The unrespecting, ruthless ocean,
   Full of fickleness and motion,
   Was guilty now of trickery which
   Was blacker than the hue of pitch.

[20]

108 They scarce had sailed two hours before
New winds stirred up the ocean more.
The sands were tossed up to the heaven,
And scared the oldest sailor even.

109 The anchors were of no avail.
They would not hold; nor could they sail
Upon their course; no pilot knew
How best to steer, or what to do.

110 The rudder broke. They knew not whether
They sailed to east or west. That weather
Bent all the masts down to the bow.
Save us, O Father, from such woe!

111 Exactly as it pleased the Lord
The ships sank with all men on board.
The life of not one man was spared
Except the king, for whom God cared.

112 Good fortune 'twas it pleased the Lord
To send to hand a piece of board.
Bruises, rags, torn shoes were his
Before he reached Pentapolis.

113 When the sea cast him ashore
The good man fell and knew no more.
Two days he knew not anything,
For he was bruised from battering.

114 The King of Glory now was kind,
And He restored the poor man's mind.
He cried, recalling the wild sea,
"Ah, I was born for misery!

115 "I lived in honor as a king,
Yet I sought trouble traveling.
Seeking a bride, I made a foe
And I returned with naught but woe.

116 "As if this were too little sadness,
Then I left Tyre in hopeless madness.
Had I there waited God's decree,
No one would now shed tears for me.

117 "But even after I left Tyre
Tarsus gave all I could desire,
For had I been the natives' brother
We could not more have loved each other.

118 "Why did I leave? It was the devil
Who moved me thus, to do me evil.
It was his sport thus to annoy me,
With many tortures to destroy me.

119 "He plotted with the ocean tides.
The winds all aided him besides.
It seemed as if Antiochus
Had urged them to torment me thus.

120 "A man should never trust the sea,
　　For it has little loyalty.
　　Its good face is hypocrisy.
　　It soon puts one in jeopardy."

121 While he was thus his fortune blaming,
　　Weeping, and of his woes complaining,
　　He saw a man who busily
　　Was casting nets into the sea.

122 The poor and ragged king with shame
　　Slowly toward the fisher came.
　　"God keep you!" he first said at meeting.
　　The fisherman returned his greeting.

123 "Friend," said the king, "you plainly see
　　That I am without property.
　　May God bless you if 'tis your will
　　To try to understand my ill.

124 "Though now I'm bruised and shivering,
　　In Tyre I was a wealthy king.
　　My people's love was copious.
　　My name is Apollonius.

125 "An honored, happy king was I.
　　I lived in ease in days gone by,
　　Yet thought myself inferior
　　Because I had not traveled more.

126 "I went abroad to seek a mate,
   But I came home in wretched state.
   Had I stayed home from Antioch
   The ocean would not me now mock.

127 "I left my kin, and I took flight;
   A fool, I boarded ship at night.
   We had good winds. Luck helped our band.
   We soon reached Tarsus, pleasant land.

128 "Those folk were full of charity.
   Toward us they showed humility.
   And when we left, I tell you truth,
   Unbidden, they showed signs of ruth.

129 "We launched with weather fair enough,
   But in short time the sea grew rough.
   All that I owned is in that sea.
   Only my life I kept with me.

130 "Vassals who chose to share my fate
   Are lost, and all my costly plate;
   Lost, through my sin, my treasured jewels,
   My horses, palfreys, and my mules.

131 "God knows in this I do not lie.
   From agony one does not die,
   Yet gladly dead I'd be, I say,
   Were it not for the Judgment Day!

132 "But since God brought me to this state,
    To pray for alms is now my fate.
    I pray you now advice to give
    How it were best for me to live."

133 And now the king kept silence. So
    The fisher spoke like one in woe.
    "King," said he then, "this much I see.
    Affliction could not greater be.

134 "In this world things are fickle ever.
    They change each day, are quiet never.
    To shift our lot is the world's care,
    Despoil the clothed, and clothe the bare.

135 "Men who their lives with ventures fill
    Must take good fortune and take ill.
    Luck's many shifts, they must take all,
    And bear whatever may befall.

136 "What fortune is men would not know
    Unless they suffered loss and woe.
    But when they've tried joys and disasters,
    They trust the Lord and become masters.

137 "He who makes you poor and ill
    Can make you wealthy, if He will.
    Fate will not give you wholly over.
    Soon your wealth you will recover.

138 "But I will share with you. I pray
    That you will be my guest today.
    Though my one robe is thin and frayed,
    I'll share with you and count me paid."

139 He split his garment with his sword,
    And took the king to his own board.
    Though he gave all he had in store,
    The king had often eaten more.

140 At dawn the king rose to depart;
    Thanking the man with all his heart,
    He promised, when once more a king,
    To pay him twice for everything.

141 "You have shown me, host, great pity.
    Now show, I pray, the road to the city,
    For the sake of God and courtesy."
    The good man told him willingly.

142 He said, "'Tis well that way to fare.
    Good men will give you robes to wear.
    If others will not help, indeed,
    For what I have you shall not need."

143 His blessèd host without delay
    Then showed him a well-traveled way.
    The king walked to the city gate.
    Shame made him loiter there and wait.

144 Now as it was about midday,
   Some young men came outside to play.
   They tossed a ball from one to the other
   As they were wont to play together.

145 The king then joined them in their game,
   Clasping his robe to hide his shame.
   He played the game as well, in truth,
   As if he had played it from his youth.

146 Straight and true he clubbed the ball,
   And when he caught, it did not fall.
   He played the game so skillfully,
   All saw a serf he could not be.

147 Architrastes, a good king,
   Now came out the ball to fling.
   All brought their bats and clubs along.
   The bats were splendid, straight and strong.

148 The stranger's play was marked by all,
   How he could bat and catch the ball.
   And Architrastes judged that he
   Kept the advantage skillfully.

149 He liked the way he caught and threw;
   His aim was accurate and true.
   Architrastes wished to play
   A game with him without delay.

150 The king then stopped the others. All
    Watched the two of them play ball.
    The stranger sometimes with a sigh
    Wiped a tear out of his eye.

151 Architrastes liked the game.
    He guessed his rival a man of fame.
    He said, "My friend, 'tis my desire
    That you shall eat before my fire."

152 The stranger did not wish to go.
    He felt great shame, could not say no.
    All asked him, spite of his poor dress.
    That he was shipwrecked they could guess.

153 And now 'twas time to eat at noon.
    The king went in, and very soon
    The others went inside the gate,
    And for their mates they did not wait.

154 Because he had no festive dress
    Apollonius felt distress.
    He stood outside. His shame was deep,
    And at the door he had to weep.

155 The king went in and took his chair,
    Then saw the other was not there.
    He called his squire and bade him bring
    The stranger who was loitering.

156 The squire found Apollonius,
   Then told the king the case was thus:
   In shipwreck he'd lost all he had,
   And would not enter poorly clad.

157 The king told them to give this guest
   Suitable robes, the very best.
   They led him to the dais then
   Among the other youthful men.

158 The king then made this exhortation:
   "Choose the place that fits your station.
   Use the judgment you should show,
   Since your rank we do not know."

159 The stranger looked at the young men,
   And would not sit in midst of them.
   He chose the king's right side at last.
   The king then ordered his repast.

160 In the palace hall they ate with zest.
   The busy servants took no rest.
   But Apollonius fasted. He
   For tears could neither eat nor see.

161 The king said, for he understood,
   "My friend, lamenting does no good.
   But if God saw you cheerful, then
   He soon would give you aid again."

162 King Architrastes, to make cheer,
    Bade his daughter to come here.
    Luciana did not loiter.
    She was a most obedient daughter.

163 The princess came in finest vesture,
    Kissed the king's hands with courtly gesture,
    And greeted all the court, who well
    Were pleased that matters thus befell.

164 When she saw Apollonius,
    She wondered who and whence he was.
    "Child," said the king, "a traveler he,
    Who bats the ball most skillfully.

165 "He played fairly, pleased me well;
    But who he is I cannot tell.
    He has escaped from death at sea,
    Where he has suffered grievously.

166 "Daughter, it would please me well,
    Could you persuade that man to tell
    About his life and ancestry,
    That we may treat him properly."

167 Gladly, as he did command her
    She approached that man with candor.
    Her words showed cordiality
    And love of good, and courtesy.

168 "You are a coward, friend," said she.
   "Though you are in this company,
   No signs of joy are on your face.
   It seems to me that proves you base.

169 "Long grief ill fits your high degree
   If you are of good family.
   Remembering woes past all redress
   Betrays some lack of manliness.

170 "All say you speak as schooled men do.
   The king, I see, is pleased with you,
   And yet you wear upon your face
   Sad looks that rob it of its grace.

171 "Now since you are in such deep woe
   It would be kind to let me know
   Your name, that I may tell the king,
   And tell him of your life something."

172 The stranger did not hesitate.
   He said, "You make my grief more great.
   I lost my name at sea. In Tyre
   My kin could tell all you desire."

173 She thought full answer was not made.
   She said, "As you would wish God's aid,
   Tell me the name by which they greet you
   That we may know how we should treat you."

174 Then Apollonius spoke again.
   He sighed and told about his pain,
   His name, his royalty, his land.
   The girl was glad to understand.

175 He told all this and more beside.
   The king and girl were gratified.
   Then Apollonius wept with pain,
   Living his past woes through again.

176 "Child, by your faith," then said the king,
   "No wonder he is sorrowing.
   Such straits you can know nothing of.
   But treat him well, if me you love.

177 "You made him weep; you made him sad.
   Now think how you can make him glad.
   Please him; he has high reputation.
   Be not afraid, but use discretion."

178 They made a place for her, and she
   Then tuned her rebeck skillfully.
   She dropped her cloak. Her tunic shone.
   Her song was one that was unknown.

179 Her lovely songs she sang and played.
   At times she hushed her voice and made
   The rebeck speak. One knew not whether
   It spoke or she; both sang together.

180 The courtiers praised her, every one.
   Her voice was like the rebeck's tone.
   She sang another melody
   With even lovelier harmony.

181 All men but Apollonius spoke.
   Within the king then wonder woke.
   He said he marvelled much that he
   With all the rest should not agree.

182 Then Apollonius answered frankly,
   "I'd not dispraise your daughter rankly,
   But if I had the strings, you'd see
   I'd touch the rebeck differently.

183 "Your daughter plays it well in part.
   Her teacher's good. She's made a start.
   But she has much to master still.
   If I should sing, she would show ill."

184 She said, "If you wish God above
   To bless you, if your friends you love,
   You must now play rebeck or harp,
   Else are your words both rude and sharp."

185 The stranger bowed to her decree.
   He tuned the rebeck skillfully.
   But then he said he knew not how
   To play with no crown on his brow.

186 This gave the king great happiness.
　　It seemed the other's grief grew less.
　　Then was brought forth his richest crown
　　And on the player's head pressed down.

187 Then when the king of Tyre was crowned,
　　He felt his sorrows mostly drowned.
　　His head grew clear, his face less pale,
　　Yet grief did not entirely fail.

188 To the girl's face his eyes he lifted.
　　She felt ashamed and her gaze shifted.
　　And then the bow he smoothly drew.
　　For joy she scarce knew what to do.

189 Sweet were the sounds beneath his bow.
　　He sang with pulsing tremolo.
　　He gladdened all their hearts but one.
　　She felt sharp pain through her heart run.

190 All said that Apollonius
　　Must match Apollo or Orpheus,
　　And the girl's song was naught to this.
　　'Twas nothing when compared with his.

191 King Architrastes was as glad
　　As if a new-won land he had.
　　He cried, "Not since my life began
　　Have I seen such a gentleman."

192 "Sire," said the girl, "at your request
I played the rebeck for our guest,
Because you wished to give him cheer.
Say, are you pleased? I wish to hear."

193 "Daughter," he said, "as your reward
He shall instruct you. From your hoard
Now give this man some costly treasure
That I gave you, to give him pleasure."

194 Soon as she knew her father pleased,
She gayly spoke; her heart was eased;
"Friend, you have pleased the king today.
I'll be your pupil, and I'll pay

195 "Two hundred talents of pure gold
And silver and servants, to have and hold.
With wholesome food and native wine
I'm sure you will no longer pine."

196 Apollonius, pleased that he
Had won success so easily,
Taught her with alacrity.

197 Not long the lessons went on thus
Ere she loved Apollonius.
Love consumed her like a fire,
And she fell ill with her desire.

198 And doctors could not give her aid;
   Although they had long study made
   Of medicine, they could not see
   How to cure her malady.

199 Her sickness grieved the court because
   No one could understand its cause.
   And Apollonius was distracted.
   Never had he felt more afflicted.

200 For his dear child 'twas natural
   That the king's hot tears should fall,
   But he controlled his heavy grief
   And in his guest's love found relief.

201 One day the king thought he would ride
   To market by the ocean-side.
   He summoned Apollonius
   To pass the morning with him thus.

202 Friendly, he took him by the hand.
   Peasants were working on the sand
   And peasant women, pleasing each.
   They left the market for the beach.

203 Thus going, by each other stayed,
   They met three youths, richly arrayed:
   Three kings' sons they, bred royally.
   They greeted them most courteously.

204 Each upon the self-same quest
   Was in this country as a guest.
   Each had wished for the king's daughter,
   And in marriage now each sought her.

205 "King," they said, "We came to you
   Once long ago your child to woo.
   You did not answer then. Today
   We come to hear what you will say.

206 "We are resolved to be content,
   Whichever man wins your assent.
   We will abide by your decree.
   The losers will leave quietly."

207 The king said, "Friends, sagaciously
   You made your plans thus to agree,
   And yet your plan may likely fail
   Because the princess now is ill.

208 "The girl has been too close a student.
   Her zeal for study was imprudent.
   Now she has come to such a state
   That for her life we're desperate.

209 "But now I think it would be better
   For each to write a suitor's letter.
   Write down your names and make it clear
   What bride-gifts you are bringing here."

210 Then each composed a formal note;
    With his own hand his name he wrote,
    Described his hills and plains and town,
    And told of his grandsires' renown.

211 They gave their letters to the king,
    Who sealed them with his signet ring;
    Apollonius he made messenger
    To take the maiden's notes to her.

212 He carried out the king's command;
    He took the letters in his hand.
    The girl, who thought he came enamored,
    Tried not to show how her heart clamored.

213 "Master," she said, "It is not clear
    Why at this hour you have come here,
    For this is not the time of day
    At which you taught me how to play."

214 "Daughter," said Apollonius,
    Who understood her, "I come thus
    Not to give lessons, but I bear
    A message to you, rich and rare.

215 "The king went out some sport to meet
    Until it should be time to eat.
    Three princes of most royal carriage
    Approached, who seek your hand in marriage.

216 "Your father knew just how to greet them,
But not with what reply to meet them.
He bade each tell for what he sues
In writing. Now you are to choose."

217 Weakly she took the letters then.
She read them once, and twice again,
But still the name did not appear
Of him she'd make her husband dear.

218 She said, with sighs of deep desire,
"Good Apollonius, King of Tyre,
My marriage may depend on you.
Do these please you? What is your view?"

219 He wisely soothed her melancholy:
"To be unhappy would be folly,
And greater folly to undo
What's best for both the king and you.

220 "I have taught you all I know.
All praise you for the skill you show.
If you become a prince's bride,
Your honor will fill me with pride."

221 "Master," she said, "your love is naught.
You'd give me up, and all you've taught.
I had not thought that day to see
When Tyre's king showed disdain toward me."

222 With wax she sealed the letter and
   Placed it in Apollonius' hand
   To give the king, still by the sea.
   He made that journey speedily.

223 Then these words met her father's sight.
   (Most skillfully the girl could write.)
   That man she'd have her husband be
   Who had been rescued from the sea.

224 The king could not think what this meant.
   He did not guess the note's intent.
   He asked the youths which one was he
   Who had escaped an angry sea.

225 One of them said, and thought it sly
   ("Eagle" the nickname he went by)
   " 'Twas I, I want it understood.
   I floated on a piece of wood."

226 Another said, "That is a lie;
   You cannot fool me. You and I
   From childhood lived together. You
   Did no such thing. It is not true."

227 While thus they spoke with tempers high,
   The king knew well that was a lie;
   But, as a most sagacious man,
   He now conceived a clever plan.

228 He turned and showed his friend the letter,
   Hoping he'd understand it better.
   When he saw what the letter said,
   Apollonius' face grew red.

229 King Architrastes noticed this
   And in his heart felt sudden bliss.
   Round his friend's neck his arm he laid,
   And privately to him he said:

230 "I beg of you, tutor and friend,
   By our love (may it never end)
   That you express to me your view;
   Else I shan't give a fig for you."

231 Then Apollonius answered, "King,
   This note gives me great suffering,
   For it may anger you. I see
   The writer must refer to me."

232 The king said, like a loyal man,
   "I cannot lie as traitors can.
   If she loves you, that pleases me,
   And I approve unstintedly."

233 Ending their talk, they joined the others.
   Then Architrastes said, "My brothers,
   I'll not encourage rivalry;
   Seek elsewhere opportunity."

234 At home, ignoring noonday fare,
   The king now climbed his daughter's stair.
   She, when she saw her father near,
   Began to tremble with her fear.

235 "Father," she panted timidly,
   "Why have you come at noon to me?
   I'm sick at heart because I know
   Your food was ready long ago."

236 He said, "Feel no anxiety.
   Only your illness troubles me.
   I bid you make an answer true;
   Whom do you wish to marry you?"

237 "Father, I will tell you clearly.
   I love King Apollonius dearly.
   If you to me another give,
   I'll never walk long as I live."

238 "Great joy, my child, to me you've given.
   Your wise choice is a gift from heaven.
   All that you wish I give to you.
   We love the man because you do."

239 The king descended, and he saw
   In the gateway his son-in-law.
   Of love they took a solemn vow.
   The princess' health grew better now.

240 The wedding feasts were rich and rare,
    And many guests were summoned there.
    The feasting lasted many a day,
    And long remained in memory.

241 The bride and bridegroom felt great love,
    And they were blessed by God above.
    No man loved woman nor woman man
    With greater love since time began.

242 One day they went to the sea-side,
    Apollonius and his bride.
    For seven months they had been married.
    Since the first week, a child she'd carried.

243 They would have turned back on that day,
    Had they not seen a ship aweigh,
    Most richly fitted, of great worth.
    The king asked whence it had set forth.

244 He asked the master in command
    To tell the name of his homeland.
    On deck, a sailor said, "We roam
    From port to port, but Tyre's our home."

245 The king said, "That's my homeland, too."
    The sailor said, "That can't be true."
    The king said, "If you wish, I'll give
    You proofs that's where I used to live."

246 The sailor said 'twould please him well:
"Since you're so positive, pray tell
If Apollonius you would know."
"As I would know myself, even so."

247 "Should you see him," said the mariner,
"Or find him through some sorcerer,
Never a soldier or a lord
Has won a prize like your reward.

248 "Tell him Antiochus is dead,
Likewise his child whom the devil led.
One stroke of Satan killed them thus;
The new king is Apollonius."

249 Joyful the king turned to his queen.
He said, "Your doubt in me I've seen.
I would not have you think me liar,
But I long cherished this desire.

250 "Since God gives me this victory
And vengeance on my enemy,
I wish to take it from the Lord,
For Antioch's no small reward."

251 "Sir," said his lady, "I am worried.
For seven months a child I've carried.
I am not fit to sail at sea
Till after my delivery.

252 "I think, if God will grant the boon,
   That my delivery will be soon.
   If you were far across the sea,
   You should come back to comfort me.

253 "But if instead you wish to wait,
   Then take me at that later date.
   I shall so suffer, if you leave me,
   That it may of my life bereave me."

254 The king said, "Queen, know certainly
   That if your father will agree,
   You shall in my realms gladly live,
   And both of them to you I'll give."

255 She begged her father: "Mercy, sire,
   Grant me now my heart's desire.
   My lord goes homeward far away;
   And I shall die, if here I stay.

256 "Antiochus, who loathed my lord,
   Has died and gone to his reward.
   My husband goes to take his throne.
   I cannot stay on here alone."

257 "Child," said the king, "'Tis well that so
   King Apollonius should go.
   Unless he wishes you to stay,
   Go, and God guide you on your way."

258 Swiftly did men the ships prepare
   With beasts and property and fare.
   For speed they greased the ships with tallow.
   Unlucky times were soon to follow.

259 The king gave, for his daughter's ease,
   Her childhood nurse, Licorides,
   And midwives; one had reputation
   Above all others in the nation.

260 He blessed the twain with his right hand.
   He prayed the Lord to bless them and
   Protect his child through heat and cold
   And safely guide her husband bold.

261 The sails were hoisted then and shifted,
   And anchors from the sands were lifted;
   The sails were bellied with the breeze
   So that the ships set out with ease.

262 Now as the ships began to sail,
   The folk began to call and wail.
   Their tears fell to the ground like dew.
   The eyes that were not wet were few.

263 Winds will not stop though people weep.
   They blew the ships upon the deep.
   They drove the ships till they no more
   Were visible to those on shore.

264 The right winds blew, for which they prayed,
     Yet calm was on the waters laid.
     The waves and wind wished to do right
     And make up for their former spite.

265 The sea was like a smooth highway.
     All were healthy. All were gay.
     They had no fear of evil fates,
     Forgetting grief and joy are mates.

266 When they had almost crossed the sea
     And could have reached port speedily,
     A sorry trick was played by fate.
     It never cast man in worse state.

267 Now of the queen we know that she
     Was far along in pregnancy,
     And now the trip was almost done.
     'Twas the ninth month. Her time was come.

268 Then she felt the tortures wild
     Of one who travails with first child.
     She prayed for death, would not believe
     A woman ever should conceive.

269 Yet from her womb at last was torn
     Her child, a princess safely born.
     And now the midwives carelessly
     Ignored the queen's great misery.

270 Lacking the care that she was needing,
   Her womb was clotted with its bleeding.
   Uncleansed of aftermath, she bled.
   At last they turned, and thought her dead.

271 It was a swoon. It was not death.
   She had but lost her pulse and breath.
   But since they found no sign of life,
   They thought her dead, and woe was rife.

272 They moaned aloud and cried, "O queen,
   Unlucky has this voyage been.
   Now you are dead, what can we do?
   In evil hour we part from you."

273 The pilot, hearing how they cried,
   Ran below with lengthy stride.
   He cried out in a voice of dread,
   "What has chanced here? Is someone dead?

274 "It matters not who it may be;
   Cast out the corpse into the sea.
   Stop your weeping! Don't delay!
   No corpse can in this vessel stay."

275 Apollonius said, "Be quiet.
   You speak rudely and you riot.
   This is a queen, not a poor woman.
   Bloodthirsty seem your words, inhuman.

276 "She was so kind she loved me when
    I was the poorest among men.
    She raised me up from penury,
    And matchless good she did to me.

277 "Can I abandon such a wife?
    No, better far to lose my life
    And go with her, than live and see
    Her reft from me so cruelly."

278 The pilot said, "Your words are vain.
    How can you talk in such a strain
    In such a time and place? Take care,
    Or you will rouse our wrath. Beware!

279 "For if we keep the body here,
    We'll lose the lives of all, I fear.
    Though one is dead, the child has breath.
    This is a case of life and death."

280 Apollonius must agree,
    Despite his anguished heart, that he
    Was speaking truth and not a lie.
    Already waves were rising high.

281 They embalmed the body as they could,
    And made a coffin of light wood.
    They sealed the box with wax and then
    Wrapped it in cloth once and again.

282 By the body, in her dress's fold,
The king laid forty coins of gold.
On a lead plate he etched her name,
Her rank, and land from whence she came.

283 When the service was complete,
The coffin nailed, and all made neat,
Though sorrow scratched their faces, all
Let the box in the ocean fall.

284 Three days the body floated thus,
And then it came to Ephesus.
There it was by a doctor found,
Who had a pupil most profound.

285 That he might live with greater joy
Where city noise did not annoy,
He moved here with his property.
On all sides were the hills and sea.

286 He walked the sands to enjoy the air,
A hundred pupils joined him there.
They found this box so sealed with glue
That water had not soaked it through.

287 Then to the master's house they bore it.
He called a smith, who pried and tore it.
They found the lady, as you know.
The master wept for very woe.

288 They found a girl with shapely face
   And rich-robed body full of grace.
   Great wealth was in the coffin, too,
   But whence it all came no one knew.

289 Then in a corner they could see
   The tablets etched most curiously.
   The master vowed that he'd fulfill
   These orders, lest he come to ill.

290 The letter was engraven thus:
   "Pity King Apollonius.
   Entomb this queen, I pray, as we
   Can't bury her in this wild sea.

291 "Take half the money here for pay,
   But give the church the rest, to pray
   For the lady's soul. More willingly
   The boys will chant the psaltery.

292 "And if you do not as I say,
   May God take all your peace away."
   "Thus may God all my life embitter
   If I do not all this and better,"

293 This was what the doctor said.
   He placed her on a priceless bed,
   And paid her honor, as was right.
   Who would not, save a man of spite?

294 When funeral plans were all prepared,
And the tomb built, with no cost spared,
The wisest pupil of the physician
Came to his house and sought admission.

295 The master said, "It pleases me
That you have come so luckily.
We're holding a strange funeral.
But you have heard about it all.

296 "Since God sent you on the right day,
Stay till this corpse is laid away.
Honor this corpse with deed and word,
And take your share of the reward.

297 "For goodness' sake and love of me
Take balsam now, and skillfully
Anoint the corpse. I'm sure that we
A nobler one shall never see."

298 The scholar, who had utmost skill,
Threw off his cloak, and with a will
Took balsam to anoint the dead,
And then approached the funeral bed.

299 He had her robe removed, then he
Took off her fine clothes carefully.
No other man could do as well.
At such work he was nonpareil.

300 All was arranged with utmost care.
   Now when the good man made a prayer
   And touched her breast, then he could see
   She died in her birth-agony.

301 He rubbed the body, hands, and feet.
   He felt the pulse. It seemed to beat.
   He tried all tests with utmost skill;
   He thought some life might be there still.

302 To the other at the door he said,
   "Although we thought this woman dead,
   I do not think my judgment bad,
   And I find signs that make me glad.

303 "I can feel her breathing stir;
   Her soul has not gone out from her.
   She's in a swoon from lack of care;
   But I can save the life that's there."

304 The master said, "Wise words, my son.
   No man has said a better one.
   Do this. You'll gain celebrity.
   The best of doctors you will be.

305 "Your famous name will never perish.
   I'll always honor you and cherish
   Your fame throughout your life, and when
   You die, you'll still be praised by men."

306 The corpse was carried where he dwelt.
    He could work better there, he felt.
    Deadwood was used the fires to stoke,
    Because such fuel emits no smoke.

307 He laid her on the floor, on straw
    And richest quilts. He bade them draw
    Her sleeve across her face for fear
    The fire would her complexion sear.

308 Then by the fire he made a smooth
    And lukewarm unguent that would soothe.
    And then he rubbed the oil on her.
    The captive spirit seemed to stir.

309 Heavy fleeces next were oiled
    And in the unguents they were boiled.
    The body then he wrapped therein.
    This was unheard-of medicine.

310 Into her womb it penetrated,
    Melted the blood coagulated,
    And freed the smothered soul from death.
    The woman sighed and drew her breath.

311 Then the doctor felt great bliss.
    He knew his physic worked by this.
    He worked with assiduity.
    And she grew better rapidly.

312 When she could rid herself of ill,
   The master mingled with great skill
   Some oil and medicine and urged
   That she drink all, and she was purged.

313 Her eyelids opened to the day.
   She spoke not, knew not where she lay.
   He was in anguish till he heard
   At last the woman speak a word.

314 In God's own time (a long time that)
   In mewing voice, weak as a cat,
   She cried, "Where can my husband be?
   He loves his shoe as much as me."

315 At last her senses all returned.
   Her lovely eyes on them she turned.
   No husband here, no serving-maid;
   The strange place made her feel afraid.

316 "Friend," she said to the physician,
   "Why am I here in this condition?
   From my dear ones I'm separated.
   Without God's aid I'm desolated.

317 "Good man, I'll not hide anything.
   I am the daughter of a king,
   And I am a king's wife also.
   I tremble now with fear and woe."

318 The pupil spoke most suitably:
"Madam, have no anxiety.
Thanks to the Lord, your pains are over.
You now will be more strong than ever.

319 "Be still, I'll ask for nothing other.
I'll treat you as I would my mother.
You'll swoon if you give way to grief,
And nothing then can give relief."

320 The woman hushed. No more she talked.
Then to his master's house he walked.
"Master, I bring good news," said he.
"The woman's cured. Come now and see."

321 He gladly went as was desired.
The woman was alive, but tired.
He told his pupil straightway there
He had no equal anywhere.

322 They cared for her till she could rise.
No treatment ever was so wise.
In a fine book it should be kept,
For it was wondrously adept.

323 The doctor made her well, then he
Made her his daughter legally.
He saved her money for her and
Not one coin of it would spend.

324 That she might live the more secure,
They had a convent built for her.
Until God brought her husband, later,
There she worshipped her Creator.

325 Now let the convent serve her needs;
Let her serve God and say her beads
While we seek Apollonius,
Who suffered woes most piteous.

326 After his wife was lost at sea
He led a life of misery;
His tears had never ceased to flow.
Each day he still felt hopeless woe.

327 The grieving band, and widowed king
Sailed on, cursing and sorrowing.
But on the waters moved God's Ghost,
Who guided them to Tarsus' coast.

328 Apollonius then went secretly
(Having no wish that men should see
His face and know how sad he felt)
Where Strangilus, his old host, dwelt.

329 When he this place revisited,
The joy he used to feel was fled.
He frightened the girl-servants badly
Because he greeted them so sadly.

330 Not one of all their friends, the men
Who left with him, was here again.
He spoke no courteous phrases. Dazed
He seemed. The maids were all amazed.

331 The babe was brought, a few days old,
In robes embroidered in fine gold.
And Luciana's wet-nurse came;
Licorides they called her name.

332 His hostess said, "I beg of you,
Where is your handsome retinue?
Not one of all who went away
With you seems to be here today.

333 "It seems that all your fortunes change.
We hardly know you. You seem strange.
You seem afflicted, bowed with woe.
For God's sake tell us all you know."

334 When Apollonius answered, he
Began to weep most copiously.
He told how in the storm's commotion
His men were all drowned in the ocean.

335 He told how he escaped from this
And came, bruised, to Pentapolis.
And how he sang, and married too,
And left with a large retinue.

336 He told how they sailed on with mirth
    Till his wife perished in childbirth,
    And what they did when she was dead,
    And how he had this child instead.

337 Then sharing Apollonius' pain,
    With grief his hosts seemed half insane.
    They wept aloud in misery
    To show the dead queen courtesy.

338 When long enough they'd sorrowed thus,
    The host to Apollonius
    Said, "King, will you a favor do
    And hark to what I say to you?

339 "This world's state, as yourself have proved,
    Stays never a long time unmoved.
    Fate gives and then it takes away,
    Not caring who is sad or gay.

340 "You've bought this knowledge very dearly.
    You know it well, if you think clearly.
    Never had man more loss and pain.
    Next comes the turn of joy and gain.

341 "One's woe cannot outlast the day
    That Fate ordains it go away.
    One should not grieve when joy is over,
    For naught by grief he can recover.

342 "We all have grieved, as you have seen.
We would have honored such a queen.
But since we were not fortunate,
We now must try our woe to abate.

343 "If tears could bring her through childbirth,
Then with our tears we'd soak the earth.
But we must grieve in vain, as she
Did for her grandsire's memory.

344 "We have a daughter like the mother,
In place of one we'll guard the other.
She is a part of our dear queen.
Nothing we lose, it may be seen."

345 The king then said, and wiped his eyes,
"Host, God we must not criticize.
Whatever He ordains must be.
To what He sends we must agree.

346 "I'll leave my daughter, if you please,
Also her nurse Licorides.
Till I've arranged her marriage, ne'er
Shall scissors touch my nails or hair.

347 "Till this is done, 'tis my desire
Not to rule Antioch or Tyre.
Nor will I rule Pentapolis.
In Egypt I will live till this."

348 He left his darling little child;
   And left her wealth and robes high piled.
   He set out on the sea that day.
   For thirteen years he stayed away.

349 The child was reared by Strangilus
   And Dionisa, her who was
   His wife. They gave her coats of fur,
   Sables, and made fine shirts for her.

350 They loved the girl and felt elation
   When she began her education
   At seven years, for she was sharp
   As knives at grammar and the harp.

351 She was beloved by all the city,
   For once her father showed them pity.
   I'll tell her name with verity.
   'Twas Tarsiana, certainly.

352 When she had reached twelve years of age,
   She was accomplished, she was sage.
   No other girl was half so fair.
   She was beloved everywhere.

353 She studied every single day.
   She did not wish to rest or play.
   Her conscience would not let her shirk.
   She knew success comes through hard work.

354 About the third hour of the day
When other children rushed away
To lunch, she did not go so fast.
Her lesson learned, she went at last.

355 She found her nurse Licorides
Afflicted with a grave disease.
Tarsiana, though she was not fed,
Stayed lovingly beside the bed.

356 "Child," said Licorides, "now I
Must ask you this before I die.
Who seem to you your father and
Your mother? What your fatherland?"

357 "Tarsus my land; I know no other,
And Dionisa seems my mother,
And Strangilus my sire. I know
No cause to think that is not so."

358 "Child," said Licorides to her,
"If you think this is true, you err.
Far nobler is your family.
I lie not. Listen now to me.

359 "Your birthplace is Pentapolis,
Where Architrastes ruler is.
It was his daughter, Luciana,
Who was your mother, Tarsiana.

360 "And Apollonius, your sire,
    Was the courageous king of Tyre,
    But he went far away and strays,
    A palmer, through Egyptian ways."

361 She told her all the tale, how he
    In luckless hour had sailed the sea,
    How Luciana he had married
    And how she in her youth was buried;

362 And how he vowed that he would win
    A husband who would please his kin
    For his child. Till her bridal morn
    His nails and hair should be unshorn.

363 When she had told this story and
    Had made the girl well understand
    And learn the names, she lost her voice,
    And she took leave of earthly joys.

364 When her nurse's soul was gone,
    Her ward, the princess, then put on
    Her shroud, and honored well the dead
    With candles and with funeral bread.

365 And now the princess Tarsiana
    Grew so perfect in her manner
    That all of Tarsus loved her dearly
    As a mother could have loved her, nearly.

366 Dionisa went, one day,
   With her along a public way,
   And Dionisa's daughter, who
   Was just the princess' age, went too.

367 The princess roused great wonderment,
   And people said where'er they went
   That the other two in loveliness
   Were worth about a pod, or less.

368 Then envy filled the wife with evil
   And she took counsel with the devil.
   She longed to bring about great ill.
   She listened to the devil's will.

369 She longed to kill the girl. She thought
   She'd not be by her father sought
   And Dionisa would take her treasure.
   No other thought would give her pleasure.

370 Then in her heart the murderess said,
   "If only this young girl were dead,
   Her ornaments my child could wear,
   And I could make a match for her."

371 While the false woman plotted treason,
   She called a slave, for she had reason
   To think if she'd free him from jail,
   He'd murder cheaply, without fail.

372 He was Theophilus. You'll see
   His name inscribed in history.
   The wicked woman thought he'd know
   How to plot a fatal blow.

373 She called him in most secretly
   And told her will and said that he
   Would surely be released from jail
   If in her plot he did not fail.

374 But the slave asked her, full of doubt,
   How her plan could be worked out.
   He'd kill the girl, she told the slave,
   When she went to her nurse's grave.

375 The slave, desiring to be free,
   Went to the grave where she might be.
   While she sang psalms he'd take her life,
   He thought, and sharpened up his knife.

376 The girl, soon as she rose from bed,
   Went with her candle and her bread
   And incense to the grave, and she
   Prayed there with great humility.

377 While the pious girl thus prayed,
   The slave stole out from ambuscade;
   He drew his sword and seized her hair,
   With full intent to kill her there.

378 "Friend," she said, "I've not hurt you,
    Or given you cause this deed to do.
    And nothing from my death you'll win
    Save consciousness of mortal sin.

379 "But if I can't escape your sword,
    Yet grant that I may pray the Lord.
    You have much time. Be not afraid.
    No one is coming to my aid."

380 Touched a little by this plea,
    He said, "I'll do that happily,"
    But said her prayers must be brief,
    For very soon she'd come to grief.

381 The girl knelt and began to cry,
    "O Lord, who rulest sun and sky,
    Who causest the moon's change to be,
    Save me by land, or save by sea.

382 "Parentless I have been reared.
    I've nothing of my father heard.
    A martyr's death to me is sent.
    If 'tis Thy will, I am content.

383 "Yet, Lord, if justice Thou wouldst do,
    (Though I deserve it not, 'tis true)
    Before this villain comes to slay
    Me thus, O send some aid, I pray!"

384 While Tarsiana thus was praying,
    Bewailing the impending slaying,
    God took pity on her there,
    Sent her aid, and heard her prayer.

385 Theophilus impatiently
    Brandished his sword. But from the sea
    Pirates appeared. They shouted, "Wait!"
    The loud noise made him hesitate.

386 Toward the shore they rowed their galley
    To kill that man. They did not dally.
    Theophilus, in deathly fright,
    Ran toward the town with all his might.

387 He went to Dionisa. He
    Was pallid with anxiety.
    "Madam," he said, "I have obeyed.
    Now set me free and have me paid."

388 The woman's answer made him hate her.
    She said, "Depart from me, false traitor!
    You have committed treachery
    And murder. I'll not set you free.

389 "Go to your village and your work.
    Else for His wrath the Lord will mark
    Your soul. Unless you swiftly hide,
    You'll die as Tarsiana died."

390 The wretch knew he had been deceived.
   He felt remorse, was deeply grieved.
   He died in slavery. In this way
   Such acts are paid for every day.

391 Although the pirates chased him fast,
   They lost Theophilus at last.
   They, when they could not reach the churl,
   Vented their rage upon the girl.

392 Liking her beauty very well,
   They thought they'd bear her off to sell.
   Through that transaction they might be
   Wealthy and free from poverty.

393 The poor girl, born in luckless hour,
   Entered the ship. They dipped the oar,
   And fearing ambush they rowed fast,
   And Mytilene reached at last.

394 They took the girl to the market-square.
   The seller had his wallet there.
   Buyers came with thought of vice.
   They longed for her at any price.

395 Antinagoras, whose power
   Controlled the city, at this hour
   Beheld her, and in mad desire
   Bid ten pounds first, and would bid higher.

396 A man came who was a procurer.
    He very much wished to secure her.
    He doubled what the lord would pay,
    Thinking to hire her in vile way.

397 Antinagoras offered thirty;
    The wicked man said he'd give forty.
    Antinagoras raised to fifty.
    The filthy sinner raised to sixty.

398 And then the wretch made his bid higher;
    If 'twas the auctioneer's desire,
    He would add twenty pounds of gold
    To any other bid there told.

399 Antinagoras then gave way.
    He thought he'd let the villain pay
    For her, then to his house he'd go
    And hire her. He'd save money so.

400 He paid for her, this wretch inhuman,
    He who would not protect a woman.
    And on his house-door he displayed
    The price of her, in evil trade.

401 The sign proclaimed to man and boy:
    "A pound of gold it costs to enjoy
    The virgin first. The rest will pay
    An ounce to see her any day."

402 When the procurer thus had planned,
The girl began to understand.
She prayed to God most piteously:
"O Lord, I trust myself to Thee.

403 "By Thy might from Theophilus,
Whose purpose was most treacherous,
My life was saved. O grant that vile
Men now may not my soul defile."

404 Now Antinagoras, the king,
Just at this time was bargaining
To buy the girl's virginity.
He asked it for God's charity.

405 'Twas granted she should be caressed
First by the prince. So, richly dressed,
With a great following she went
Toward the vile brothel, ill-content.

406 And there was Tarsiana left.
The lamb was with the wolf. Bereft
Of all else but her wits, she now
Tried to find mercy anyhow.

407 She fell at his feet piteously,
Crying, "Have mercy! Hark to me!
If you will wait and hear, the Lord
Will bless and give you great reward.

408 "If you take my virginity,
In mortal sin we both shall be.
You'll not gain much. 'Twill ruin me,
And stain your great nobility.

409 "I'll lose my virtue, and you must
Be plunged in mortal sin through lust.
You are a great man. God will bless
You if you spare the fatherless."

410 She told him all her woes, how she
Her parents lost in infancy,
And how, since she was left much treasure,
She won her guardian's displeasure.

411 Antinagoras, though lustful,
By her long tale was made less zestful.
He turned. Respect was in his eyes,
And his words were very wise.

412 "Girl," he said, "you're telling me
That you are of good family.
I understand you well; your plea
Is just, deserving lenity.

413 "We all are mortal and must die.
Not one of us from fate can fly.
And every man should meditate.
He'll pay for sin at heaven's gate.

414 "I have a daughter of your years.
   I guard her carefully. The fears
   I'd have for her if she were you
   Now make me wish to shield you too.

415 "Besides, I'm thinking of your sire.
   I wish to grant you your desire.
   And I will grant you more, from pity,
   That you may not forget this city.

416 "The price I'd pay were I to do
   This sinful deed I'll give to you,
   Then you can bribe each man who comes
   To leave you sinless with these sums.

417 "Till your captivity is past,
   You shall have gold while mine shall last.
   Now may it be the Lord's desire
   To lift your lot in this world higher!"

418 Then Antinagoras went away.
   Another came with her to play.
   But she so wisely her case stated
   That still she was not violated.

419 All men who entered through her door
   She changed, till lust they did abhor.
   All left her her virginity,
   And yet they paid her handsomely.

420 When only half a day was past,
     The girl had so much gold amassed
     That if her keeper had but half,
     He would be moved to jest and laugh.

421 He saw her happy. She was sly,
     Wishing to deceive thereby.
     He said, "You'll have a good career,
     Since your face shows no pain nor fear."

422 The girl then asked most reasonably:
     "Sir, would you but grant it to me,
     I know another trade less sinful,
     More honorable and more gainful.

423 "If you will grant through your compassion
     That I may enter this profession,
     Then I will pay you faithfully;
     Both rich and sinless we shall be.

424 "You should use me in the way
     Which you think would most highly pay.
     Since I cost a goodly sum,
     I ought to make a high income."

425 The girl's speech was so full of art,
     It softened the procurer's heart.
     He told her she might try her scheme,
     If she her promise could redeem.

426 Then, very early the next day,
　　 She dressed in garments rich and gay.
　　 She took her harp to the market-square
　　 That she might play for money there.

427 The harpstrings and her fingers meet
　　 In notes both natural and sweet.
　　 The market could not hold the men
　　 Who climbed upon the wall-seats then.

428 When she had sung and she had played
　　 To the joy of everyone, she made
　　 A recitation. To pass time
　　 She told them all her life, in rhyme.

429 Her tale was clear. Their ears she ravished.
　　 A hundred marks on her they lavished.
　　 The wretch was pleased with her profession.
　　 It brought great wealth to his possession.

430 The people loved her past all measure,
　　 And in her singing took great pleasure.
　　 Knowing she had a wicked master,
　　 They gave their aid to her the faster.

431 Prince Antinagoras' love was best.
　　 As his own daughter she was blest.
　　 Unless he heard her sing, the flavor
　　 Went from his food. It had no savor.

432 She was so shrewd that to her master
    She brought home money fast and faster.
    With laugh and jest she brought it in,
    Yet she knew how to keep from sin.

433 As it pleased God, a long time she
    Lived thus, and yet from sin was free.
    Since she her livelihood can earn,
    To her sad sire now let us turn.

434 Since he had his departure made
    Ten years had passed. With beard in braid
    Her father came and thought to see
    His daughter grown. 'Twas not to be.

435 When he saw Apollonius,
    Pale and scared was Strangilus,
    And he rebuked his wife, but she
    Told falsehoods most ingeniously.

436 When Apollonius came near
    They hugged him hard with proper cheer.
    But then he looked to find his daughter.
    He could not be glad while he sought her.

437 "Host," said the king, "how can this be?
    Why comes my daughter not to me?
    I want the truth, and without fail.
    It seems to me you're looking pale."

438 Then Dionisa told a lie.
"O king, your daughter had to die.
A deadly sickness stopped her heart,
And from this world she did depart."

439 Then Apollonius was dumb.
For a long time no words would come.
He never had known so rude a blow.
Half stunned, he bowed his head in woe.

440 At last, after a half-day's time,
He thirsted; he would take no wine,
But drank some water; then he spoke.
His words great pity should evoke.

441 His hostess cared not, though he said,
"Hostess, I wish that I were dead.
When my wife died, I thought my child
Would make my anguish the more mild.

442 "I thought that finding her today
Would close the wound, drive woe away;
The old wound is cut deeper still.
No medicine will cure this ill.

443 "Her robes are fresh. Scant time has sped
Since my darling has been dead.
I pray you bring them to me now
To hold to my grief-stricken brow.

444 "Now take me to her tomb. I'll fold
My arms about the hard and cold
Stone monument, and voice my grief,
And in my tears find some relief."

445 Then Dionisa did great evil.
(She was a servant of the devil.)
A monument, white as a smock,
Was built, the father's grief to mock.

446 The stone was graven in this manner:
"Strangilus here laid Tarsiana,
Daughter of Apollonius.
In her twelfth year she went from us."

447 He took mementos of her then
And to his ships he bade his men
Bear them. And to the sepulcher
He went that he might mourn for her.

448 But when he reached her grave, he found
He could not weep. Though on the ground
He stretched himself, he was not sad.
His heart grew light and he felt glad.

449 Then he turned toward himself. He said,
"O God! What does this mean? If dead
My daughter lay within this place
The tears would rain down on my face.

450 "This tale is false, it now is clear.
My daughter is not buried here.
They've cast her in some evil place.
Alive or dead, God show her grace!"

451 In Tarsus he would stay no longer,
Because it made his grief the stronger.
Worn with tears, with covered head
He sought his ships. No word he said.

452 He told his men they must set sail
Toward Tyre. He felt his life-blood fail,
And in that place he wished to die,
That he among his kin might lie.

453 They raised the anchor, set each oar,
Unfurled the sails, and left the shore.
The waves were calm; the wind grew strong.
Tarsus was left behind ere long.

454 Halfway to Tyre, the quiet sea
And favoring winds changed suddenly.
In their course they could not stay,
But they were driven another way.

455 The sea was now so agitated
That they no longer navigated.
They lost the rudder. Each man said
To himself they were as good as dead.

456 The terrible tempest did not wane.
   Lashed by the deadly hurricane
   The ship was brought by the Holy King
   Where Tarsiana was suffering.

457 Thus they reached Mytilene. Tired
   And suffering, they then inquired
   What place this was. The wind subsided
   And they thanked God that He had guided.

458 They anchored ship in the roadstead,
   Relit their fire which had been dead,
   And dried their clothes. In this the king
   Found no relief nor comforting.

459 'Twas Apollonius' natal day.
   He had been wont to make it gay
   With feasting. Now he told his men
   To amuse themselves with feasts again.

460 But in the ship's far corner he
   Flung himself down and swore he'd see
   A foot cut off from any man
   Who spoke to him. This was his ban.

461 The seamen heeded his command.
   They purchased great provisions and
   Prepared the feast about midday.
   No man who came was sent away.

462 No one dared call their lord, for he
    Had fixed so harsh a penalty.
    Therefore like prudent seamen they
    Turned to their feasting and their play.

463 Now Antinagoras passing by
    In search of pastime, chanced to espy
    On shipboard all this company.
    He knew them folk of quality.

464 And when they saw him come this way,
    They begged of him that he would stay
    And with the rest partake of food.
    He sat down lest they think him rude.

465 As they sat chatting at the board,
    He asked the name of the ship's lord.
    "He's lying ill," they said, "and yet
    His sickness is but deep regret.

466 "He says if anyone shall dare
    To call him to our banquet fare,
    He shall lose one of his two feet,
    And both, should he the offense repeat."

467 When Antinagoras asked why
    The poor man should thus curse and sigh,
    The seamen told him all the truth
    Of Apollonius, from his youth.

468 He said, "Why surely that's the same
   One I've heard Tarsiana name!
   Whatever happens, I will see
   If I can make him speak to me."

469 They showed him Apollonius,
   Pleased that their guest had spoken thus.
   He saw his beard that hid his chest.
   His manner much amazed the guest,

470 Who said, "God's blessing be on you.
   I hear that you have cause to rue.
   Don't spurn me. I am a well-doer.
   I'm not a beggar or a suer."

471 The king turned over on his bed
   To see who had so little dread
   Of punishment. It was a stranger.
   Therefore the king controlled his anger.

472 The other urged him, would not leave.
   He wished to make him cease to grieve.
   He said, "O Apollonius,
   In ignorance you're acting thus.

473 "My name is Antinagoras. I
   Govern this seaport where you lie.
   I came out here to seek some sport,
   And see the boats that lie in port.

474 "When I had gone along the shore,
    I liked your fine ship more and more.
    Then all your men, greatest and least,
    Invited me to join their feast.

475 "The men were schooled and courteous.
    Their food was fine and bounteous.
    I asked which one was the ship's master.
    They told of you and your disaster.

476 "If you would but believe and hark,
    It would be best to leave this dark
    Retreat. My town could show you pleasure,
    And curb your grief to proper measure.

477 "Now change your thoughts. I think you should,
    For God even yet may send you good.
    I truly think you will win gladness
    And lose the cause of all this sadness."

478 Toward him the king now turned his face
    And said, "My friend, please leave this place.
    I know your solacing is wise.
    I know how sagely you advise.

479 "But, for my sins, I feel such rue
    That my poor heart's pierced through and through.
    Of heaven and earth I now am tired.
    Nothing is left to be desired."

480 Then Antinagoras turned and left.
　　He saw this goodly man, bereft
　　Unreasonably. Profoundly sad,
　　He said that this lord's lot was bad.

481 He said that he could make no plan
　　To straighten things for this poor man.
　　"Woe that I knew not yesterday
　　Fills me. I mean just what I say.

482 "Yet there's one scheme that might avail.
　　Nothing we lose, if we should fail.
　　If God will aid us, well I know
　　We'll soon have taken Jericho.

483 "In our town is a marvellous
　　Fair kidnapped girl. She'll come to us.
　　If she with her sweet entertaining
　　Cannot give aid, all aid is feigning."

484 To her vile master, 'twas made clear
　　He should send Tarsiana here.
　　If Apollonius was cured,
　　All that she wished would be secured.

485 She came most gorgeously attired,
　　And smiled till all their hearts were fired.
　　At her first words each man could see
　　Why she was loved exceedingly.

486 Antinagoras said, "My dear,
   God grant 'tis well that you come here.
   Now is the most important time
   To show your skill in song and rhyme.

487 "The lord of all this company,
   Of great wealth, lore, and family,
   Is crushed by a most heavy grief.
   For God's love, give him some relief."

488 She said, "Show him to me; I know
   My medicines will soothe him so
   That if he is not dead he'll eat
   And play, and feel that life is sweet."

489 To the king they then conducted her.
   She said, "God keep you, traveler.
   I grieve for you." She took her stand
   Before him then, with harp in hand.

490 "Think not my solace is disgrace.
   For you will find I am not base.
   No dancing bawd you see in me.
   I use this trade unwillingly.

491 "My parents both were honorable.
   I must not speak of them in full.
   I came to birth in the fishy sea.
   My guardians were false to me.

492 "Pirates in ships snatched me away
From one in very act to slay.
A man bought me who for a price
Often gives virgins up to vice.

493 "Yet God so guards me from this evil,
That I've not yielded to the devil.
I seek a trade by which to flee
Through some means from my infamy.

494 "If you should die, as is your will,
Of you will all mankind speak ill.
Change your abode, if you would live.
Come with me. I a cure can give."

495 She said much more. Her speech was long.
Then with her harp she sang a song.
She spoke rhymed couplets, finely made.
Some heed to all her skill he paid.

496 When she had entertained him well,
The king said to her, "I can tell
That you are of good family.
You have been taught with artistry.

497 "If the Creator it should please,
I would most gladly give you ease.
I'll free you if the man will sell.
That deed would please me very well.

498 "Now for this skill that you have shown
    I give ten pounds of gold. Be gone
    With blessing of the Lord, for I
    Shall not be cured until I die."

499 She went to Antinagoras
    And said, "His grief is as it was.
    He's offered me ten pounds for pay,
    But I will not take them away."

500 When Antinagoras was told
    He said, "No, do not take his gold.
    I'll give you twice as much as he.
    You must not work without your fee.

501 "But earnestly I beg of you,
    Go back and sing to him anew.
    Your singing is the means, I'm sure,
    By which the Lord will work his cure."

502 So Tarsiana went to sing
    And play her harp before the king.
    "Good man," she said, "until I've made
    Your fullest cure, I'll not be paid.

503 "I'll ask some riddles. If you see
    What each answer ought to be,
    I'll take the money that you owe.
    If you can't answer, I'll say no."

504 The king was hesitant, for fear
 'Twould seem he held his gold too dear
 And therefore failed to answer her.
 Some men, he felt, would so aver.

505 The girl said, "Tell me now this thing.
 What house is always murmuring,
 Though the indwellers all are dumb?
 Now please me with the answer. Come!"

506 The king said, "I'm considering.
 The house is a river murmuring.
 The inmates are the fish." "Correctly
 You speak. Now guess this one directly.

507 "The river's kin and friend am I.
 My lovely hair I raise on high.
 My trade is to make black of white.
 That one is hard to solve aright."

508 "The reed is water's kin, for where
 It flows it grows. Its lovely hair
 Grows high, and books are made of it.
 Now ask the third to test my wit."

509 "I am the forest's child most swift.
 Furrows I cut and leave no rift.
 I fight the winds. I'm dangerous."
 "Ships," said the king, "are ever thus."

510 The princess said, "To three at least
You've answered wisely as a priest.
But do not now, I pray, desist.
A cure is never worked so fast.

511 "Between two fires that burn their best
There lies a naked thing, a guest,
Untroubled by the heat or cold.
That riddle is well hid, I'm told."

512 The king replied at once, "I know it.
If I were gayer I could show it,
Stripped for the bath; but it is low
And base to speak of vile things so."

513 "I have no limbs, no parts inside,
But two teeth like an elephant goad.
The one who bears me I hold still."
"That is an anchor, I know well."

514 "I'm soft as wool, soft as a bog.
When I swell up, I'm like a frog.
I grow in water, where I plunge."
"The answer, sister, is the sponge."

515 Said Tarsiana, "I must say
That I already feel more gay.
I see good signs, if God will aid,
That a full cure may soon be made.

516 "I have three riddles easier.
    Don't be too lazy now to stir.
    Or ask me one, if you prefer."

517 "You bore me," said the king. "God bless me,
    How your persistence does distress me!
    Now if you ask me more than three,
    You'll be a liar. Don't cozen me."

518 "Downy inside, and smooth to the air,
    Inside my breast I wear my hair.
    From hand to hand I go in play.
    When men go eat, outside I stay."

519 "A ball, once in Pentapolis,
    Changed all my misery to bliss.
    King Architrastes, playing ball,
    Asked me to eat within his hall."

520 "I am not black, nor white nor red;
    No tongue by which wise saws are said
    Have I. I win when I am opposite.
    I can be bought for a small bit."

521 "Peddlers sell mirrors for a penny.
    As for their hue, they haven't any.
    One may in them his own face see.
    They conquer high and low degree."

522 "Beneath one roof four sisters we.
In pairs we follow those who flee.
We chase each other all our days
And never gain, yet we embrace."

523 "That riddle's easy to reveal.
Each of the sisters is a wheel.
Beneath a carriage, two and two,
Although they never join, they go."

524 The girl still did not wish to leave him.
As to the number she'd deceive him,
She thought, but Apollonius
Knew how to count, and he spoke thus:

525 He said, "You should be glad, my friend.
I've answered each thing to the end.
And I will give you extra pay.
Now speak no more, and go away.

526 "I see you'd make me glad and hale,
But it is needful you should fail.
I should win all men's laughter, I,
If I should break my pledge to die."

527 Nothing she could say would then
Make him want happiness again.
Saddened, not knowing what to do,
Her arms about his neck she threw.

528 Enraged, he did her grievous harm.
　　He threw her off, twisting her arm,
　　And at her face he aimed a blow
　　That from her nose caused blood to flow.

529 The poor girl then raised loud lament.
　　To all her sorrows she gave vent.
　　Would Antinagoras all had lost,
　　Rather than dined at such a cost.

530 She cried, "O wretched, wretched me!
　　Forever doomed to misery!
　　In strange lands I am cursed and flayed,
　　And for good service badly paid!

531 "Ill luck you had, poor Luciana!
　　So has your daughter, Tarsiana!
　　My birth at sea made death your portion.
　　Would that you'd killed me by abortion!

532 "My father, Apollonius,
　　Could not give you a burial place.
　　Your coffin in the sea was cast.
　　We know not where it rests at last.

533 "Life for me was very hard.
　　I was by Dionisa reared.
　　From envy she soon wished me dead.
　　O would I were!" the poor girl said.

534 "But for my sins I then was saved,
 And by my rescuers enslaved.
 My buyer had as his vile goal
 My degradation, body and soul.

535 "But Heaven helped me to escape,
 And never yet have I known rape.
 Good men have given me much gold
 So that my master will not scold.

536 "'Midst other woes this is the worst:
 A man who wished my service first
 Has shamed me with such cruelty
 As it must make God sad to see.

537 "King Apollonius, ill-fated!
 If you knew how your child is bated,
 You would avenge her and would grieve.
 But I fear you no longer live.

538 "Through my great sins I do not know
 My sire's grave nor my mother's. O!
 Beastlike, into the market-square
 I'm led, to please the base men there."

539 Then Apollonius' heart grew light.
 He understood her words aright.
 He asked (his voice with gladness broke)
 If it was utter truth she spoke.

540 "Girl, if God lets you see your sire,
Forgive me now. 'Tis my desire
To give you wealth, for though I erred,
I am not base in act or word.

541 "And now, if you can call to mind
Your nurse's name, perchance you'll find
Your father, and I'll find my daughter
With joy, after I've sadly sought her."

542 The girl forgave him graciously
And answered him with honesty:
"My nurse," she said, "I sadly miss.
Licorides the dear name is."

543 Now Apollonius' joy was wild.
He understood she was his child.
He prayed, as he rose up from bed;
"O God, Thou art the Truth," he said.

544 He embraced her, and his joy was high.
"Child, for your loss I thought I'd die!"
He cried. "Now care has gone away!
Now dawns my brightest, happiest day!

545 "I never thought that I would see
This day, or hold you lovingly.
Ah, how your loss has made me sad!
Now I thank God that I am glad."

546 And then he called, "Come here, my men!
    Your master now is well again!
    Put trappings on your horses! Dance!
    Raise targets! Strike them with the lance!

547 "Prepare a feast most sumptuous!
    For my lost child is here with us!
    God sent the storm! That storm is dear
    That drove us ignorantly here."

548 Antinagoras was as glad
    As if the whole of France he had
    Won as reward for his good ways.
    He did not do good just for praise.

549 Now Antinagoras had heard
    That Apollonius pledged his word
    Never to cut his hair or beard
    Till his child's wedding day had neared.

550 To bring his service to an end
    He now asked for the maiden's hand.
    Then would the king have no excuse
    To go unkempt, as was his use.

551 I think that Antinagoras' deeds
    Should be set down, for the king's needs
    He so well served. Were he a Christian
    We'd pray for him, beyond all question.

552 "King," Antinagoras said, "I pray,
Give me your daughter that I may
Become her husband. I have served her.
Therefore I have the more deserved her.

553 "I am fit to be your son.
You have a kingdom. I have one.
You would be surprised to hear
A better offer made this year."

554 King Apollonius said, "'Tis granted.
Your kindness shall not be repented.
You have been a loyal friend
And brought my sickness to an end.

555 "I would not cut my hair, I swore,
Nor cut my beard or nails, before
My child I to a husband gave.
She is betrothed. Now let me shave!"

556 Throughout the town the news was carried
That their lord was to be married.
Joy then reigned in every breast
Save the vile man's. He was distressed.

557 While the news rang, though she kept still,
Tarsiana did not take it ill.
For Antinagoras had been kind
In need, and she kept that in mind.

558 The day was set, the blessing made,
　　And for the bridal all men prayed.
　　So lavish was the preparation,
　　Words fail to tell of the occasion.

559 Yet Tarsiana was not sure
　　That she was even yet secure
　　Till that false traitor, her vile master,
　　By stones or sword had met disaster.

560 Therefore the city council met.
　　In a good place was the meeting set.
　　Then Antinagoras said, "Now hark.
　　I want you all my words to mark.

561 "The good king Apollonius
　　Wishes to thank each one of us.
　　A daughter that he thought was dead
　　Has been found here. You should be glad.

562 "I made proposal for her, and
　　In marriage I have won her hand.
　　All of you know her brilliancy
　　That she has proved repeatedly.

563 "Her father feels deep thanks belong
　　To you who shielded her from wrong.
　　The Lord was very kind to us
　　And from remorse He kept us thus.

564 "The king desires that you be told
Five hundred thousand marks of gold
He gives to you unstintedly.
In this you see his courtesy.

565 "Especially he begs of you
That you will kill the traitor who
Wished to defame his child, lest he
Now vaunt himself obnoxiously."

566 Then all as one they made reply:
"May that good king live happily!
Since vengeance he entrusts to us,
He shall not find us languorous."

567 Nor did they use procrastination.
They moved with righteous indignation.
They seized the traitor, bound him tight,
And stoned the wretch to death that night.

568 When they had thus avenged the king,
They tore the vile man up to fling
Him piecemeal to the dogs. They said
This fate was just for one so bad.

569 And Tarsiana husbands got
For all the girls that man had bought,
And dowries. They became sedate.
They had been most unfortunate.

570 The council thanked the king, for he
    Had treated them most handsomely.
    They wished to make some fine reward
    Commemorating this kind lord.

571 They had his life-sized image made
    Of finest gold, and they displayed
    It in the market. It showed the king
    And at his feet his fair offspring.

572 The pedestal was graven thus:
    "The wise king Apollonius
    Was driven by a tempest wild
    To our shores and here found his child."

573 Joy brought back Apollonius' health.
    A wedding gift of greatest wealth
    He gave his daughter. 'Twas the town
    Of Antioch, of great renown.

574 And he helped Mytilene then,
    For he gave alms to all the men
    Who wished them. Till the Judgment Day
    Will Mytilene for him pray.

575 Now Apollonius had desire
    With braided beard to enter Tyre.
    His boats were decked most lavishly,
    Showing his great prosperity.

576 But first to Tarsus the ships turned,
   For Dionisa must be burned,
   And her weak husband must be cast
   In jail, and justice done at last.

577 He told his pilot of his plan.
   A vision to the king came then,
   An angel all in white, all-knowing,
   And he advised against his going.

578 "Go not there, Apollonius,"
   He said, "Go first to Ephesus.
   When you have set your foot on land,
   Then I will give my next command.

579 "Ask to be shown Diana's fane.
   It stands upon a level plain.
   Its inmates wear long garbs of wool,
   One nun they Luciana call.

580 "If you come at the caller's hour
   Strike with the knocker on the door.
   The prioress will welcome you,
   And all the rest will come out too.

581 "Then look well at the abbess' mate.
   Respect her, for her worth is great.
   Ask her to lead you to the chest
   Where her family relics rest.

582 "And as she leads you there, I say
    That you must tell her on the way
    About your woes on sea and land.
    Be sure to make her understand.

583 "This will your happiness enhance
    More than winning all of France.
    Then to Tarsus you may go,
    Casting aside all youthful woe."

584 To tell more would waste time for us.
    As soon as Apollonius
    Awoke, he set to work and did
    Each thing he heard the angel bid.

585 While he related his affairs,
    Luciana could not say her prayers.
    So well she knew all that he told,
    The convent scarce her joy would hold.

586 At the king's feet in ecstasy
    She fell and cried, "O look at me!
    When you guess who I am, I know
    Your heart will lose its heavy woe.

587 "I am your wife, the one you lost,
    The one that in the sea was cast
    Because you thought her dead. In me
    King Architrastes' child you see.

588 "I am the one who loved you well.
　　Upon my bed as I lay ill
　　You brought me notes that asked my hand.
　　My answer you well understand."

589 King Apollonius understood.
　　In his elation scarcely could
　　He keep his senses. In their glee
　　They knew God gave them victory.

590 Then to the other each explained
　　What each had lost, what each had gained.
　　And for the doctor specially
　　The king felt grateful amity.

591 The princess clasped her mother and
　　They could not make her loose her hand.
　　Her husband wept like the queen's own brother.
　　They all took joy in one another.

592 The doctor then did not regret
　　That he saved Luciana. Yet,
　　Though pay was offered lavishly,
　　He sought their friendship, not a fee.

593 Great joy ran through all Ephesus.
　　All men were glad that things went thus,
　　But all the convent women cried
　　Since now their mate would leave their side.

594 The royal family then stayed
   A while, and a new nun was made
   The abbess. Then they left much money
   And went away upon a journey.

595 They sailed away across the sea;
   The Ephesians felt great misery.
   They sailed toward Tarsus very fast,
   And joyfully arrived at last.

596 Ere they could even disembark
   The council came to give them mark
   Of their high favor. Never one
   Has seen a task with such joy done.

597 They met their king with dignity,
   Singing from books and memory,
   Avowing their great love, and ruing
   All Dionisa's evil-doing.

598 On entering the city they
   Through joyful crowds must make their way.
   To all the king began to say:

599 "Listen, my people, and God bless you.
   Don't interrupt while I address you.
   If any I've wronged a penny's worth,
   Let him come now and tell it forth."

600 Then all cried, "Each of us will tell
You saved our lives. We know it well.
All that we promised once to you,
If you command it, we will do."

601 "When I came to you again,
(We'll not talk of the first time) then
I brought my tiny babe and said
Her mother we had left for dead.

602 "Her to my treacherous hosts I brought
With rich possessions, for I thought
That they would rear her. But they tried
To kill her, and they said she died.

603 "When I thought she would soon be married,
They told me she was dead and buried.
Thank God, I have her here with me,
But I long suffered agony.

604 "If you will not make due amends,
Outside your roofs our friendship ends.
Beyond forgiveness, this offends."

605 O how the council then was stirred!
They could not listen. They averred
That Dionisa must not be
Excused from heavy penalty.

606 Both Dionisa and her lord
   They placed in chains, and all their stored-
   Up wealth they seized. Then they were tried.
   It took but brief time to decide.

607 Dionisa did not know
   Of Tarsiana's coming, so
   She clung to her old story, said
   That she could prove the girl was dead.

608 But all of this was proved a lie,
   For Tarsiana with a cry
   Sprang up, and with great fluency
   Told of her great indignity.

609 To make the truth impervious
   To lies, they called Theophilus.
   Fearing to lie before the king,
   He told the truth of everything.

610 And so the council learned that day
   Just how the death was planned, what pay
   The murderer would have received.
   Then Dionisa was much grieved.

611 There was no need more time to take.
   They burned the woman at the stake
   And hanged her husband, as was meet,
   And then they all went home to eat.

612 Theophilus fared better. They,
Because he gave her time to pray,
Gave him his life and liberty,
Releasing him from slavery.

613 This done, all wished to celebrate,
While the king came in in state.
The royal party visited
A while, and then away they sped.

614 To Antioch they sailed with ease,
Because they had a favoring breeze.
As they expected, all the men
Were glad their king had come to them.

615 Their fortresses to him they gave,
And all the wealth that they could save.
The nobles gave him jewels. Woe
Betide Antiochus below!

616 To give their sureties now they vied.
Apollonius' realm spread far and wide.
Solving the riddle brought him glory,
Though for so long his lot seemed sorry.

617 When he was strong on every side
And all his subjects satisfied,
Then he announced he would withdraw,
And give the state to his son-in-law.

618 The people liked his lordship well.
　　Far wiser than was usual
　　He seemed. Their welcome made him glad.
　　He realized he was well wed.

619 When all things were established thus,
　　Then the good Apollonius
　　Set sail with all his family
　　That they Pentapolis might see.

620 King Architrastes then was glad,
　　For he had thought that they were dead.
　　Fifteen long years, since they left there,
　　Had passed, they all were well aware.

621 The citizens, the very city
　　Felt joy. They made a merry ditty
　　Out of the words, "O happy day!"
　　The streets were hung with banners gay.

622 For many years they'd had no other
　　Than this old king. He had no brother
　　Nor any son. They'd mourned for this;
　　Soon they'd have no king's hand to kiss.

623 Therefore they felt felicity.
　　No alien now their king would be.
　　And loyally they looked ahead,
　　Seeing how things would soon have sped.

624 No words can tell their happiness.
They put on their best shoes and dress,
And bathed to make their color fair,
And barbers swiftly hacked their hair.

625 Incense they burned, and meat they fried,
Game, pork, and beef, both fresh and dried.
Capons and hens were not for sale.
Each man might have one without fail.

626 Each day the people begged in prayer
That Apollonius have an heir.
God heard the prayer of everyone,
And Luciana bore a son.

627 When this young prince they had secured,
All the folk were reassured;
But joy was changed to sorrowing,
For Architrastes died, their king.

628 But let us leave this grief and woe
To those who must it undergo.
Let us go on and end our tale,
Else some will say that our wits fail.

629 When the king died, his funeral
Was fine, and rich his burial.
All of his power fitly was
Given to Apollonius.

630 Through all the woes that on him snowed,
    He still remembered thanks he owed
    The fisherman who took him in
    And shared his very cloak with him.

631 Where this man lived, the king well knew.
    He went there, saw him come in view,
    And sent men to him, ordering
    Him to appear before the king.

632 The fisher came in his poor dress.
    He still knew poverty's distress.
    But anyone might have believed
    Him count, he was so well received.

633 And he was given maids and men
    For servants, flocks and flocks again,
    And horses, woods, and vineyards too,
    And all the fields there were in view.

634 Of a whole town he was made lord.
    He had such wealth he could afford
    Never to let one of his race
    Do menial work or service base.

635 May God who reigns, the One in Three,
    Give to each man in misery
    Even such a host or such a guest,
    Who gives the other of his best.

636 To the new prince was homage paid.
   He bore the name his grandsire had.
   They trained him like a good young vine,
   And toward him made their thoughts incline.

637 Apollonius was fortunate,
   He felt, with good base for his state
   And all its future, for he saw
   He had a prudent son-in-law.

638 He prayed to the most Holy King
   That He would give them sheltering.
   Then with his queen 'twas his desire
   To go back to his native Tyre.

639 Since he had left, the folk of Tyre
   In grief had felt but one desire.
   They did not know why they were left,
   By God's will, of their lord bereft.

640 Seeing the king, they were like men
   Who are let out of jail again.
   That their eyes fooled them they had fear.
   They scarcely could believe him near.

641 Indeed he pleased them just as well
   As would the angel Gabriel.
   They were a faithful following.
   They had not taken a new king.

642 Things were in almost perfect state.
There was no quarrelsome debate.
Coffers were filled; old griefs were buried.
Young girls were now grown up and married.

643 In Tyre he ordered all to meet him.
All the rich lords came there to greet him.
He gave his lengthy story tongue,
And told why he had stayed so long.

644 All grieved to hear his misery
And all his woes on land or sea.
But since the glorious end was such,
They didn't think it mattered much.

645 They all said, "You have suffered, sire,
In your adventures, evils dire.
But now it would be best forgot,
For honor through it all was got.

646 "Antiochus, your enemy,
Has yielded you his empery.
Pentapolis obeys your son.
And Mytilene you have won.

647 "Besides, you have brought home a queen
From Tarsus, which is your demesne.
We hope, and think our hope not vain,
That your good luck will never wane.

648 "Seeking adventure here and there,
   You chose in foreign lands to fare.
   Now, sire, since all is now secure,
   You should remain at home, we're sure."

649 The king replied, "I think it well
   That I should heed the things you tell.
   Truly to speak, I now am tired,
   And I'll enjoy all I desired."

650 He lived on while God granted life.
   Sweetly he lived with his dear wife.
   And when the hour of death came, he
   Died like a king, decorously.

651* Now Apollonius has died. So all of us must die,
   However much we love ourselves. Keep that in memory.
   For what we do in life in the hereafter we must pay.
   We never shall return to earth when once we go away.

652 Another will enjoy all things that we have left behind.
   If we don't help ourselves, then no one else will help, we'll find.

---

* Quatrains 651–655 were not part of the Spanish original but were added by a copyist.

If we will always help ourselves, we'll find 'twill
make us hardy,
But help that others give to us is apt to be too
tardy.

653 Our hardships for religion's sake, long after we
have perished
Will be by every man alive still reverenced and
cherished.
Why is it that we pray the most for those now
passed away?
When we are dead, it is not they who for our
souls will pray.

654 Though we look at men's wealth and swoon
with envious despair,
We're not long grateful to the man who offers
us a share.
Why should we save our wealth for those who
live when we are dead?
They will not thank us for it, but will mock at
us instead.

655 And now let us stop talking. Let us not prolong
this tale.
Our days on earth are sparse and few, and soon
our lives will fail.

And when we die, what holy robes shall our
poor souls receive,
To wear at the great feast of God, in whom we
all believe?

656 The Lord who rules the winds and sea,
   May He our Guide and Pattern be.
   May He allow us to behave
   So that He may with mercy save.

   Let all with reason say Amen.

www.ingramcontent.com/pod-product-compliance
Lightning Source LLC
Chambersburg PA
CBHW061417300426
44114CB00015B/1970